TORONTO THE GOOD

TORONTO THE GOOD
ANDREW MOODIE

PLAYWRIGHTS CANADA PRESS
TORONTO

PLAYWRIGHTS CANADA PRESS
The Canadian Drama Publisher
215 Spadina Ave., Suite 230, Toronto, ON Canada M5T 2C7
phone 416.703.0013 fax 416.408.3402
orders@playwrightscanada.com • www.playwrightscanada.com

For professional or amateur production rights, please contact Playwrights Canada Press at the address above.

The publisher acknowledges the support of the Canadian taxpayers through the Government of Canada Book Publishing Industry Development Program, the Canada Council for the Arts, the Ontario Arts Council, and the Ontario Media Development Corporation.

 Canada Council for the Arts Conseil des Arts du Canada  ONTARIO ARTS COUNCIL CONSEIL DES ARTS DE L'ONTARIO

 Canada  Ontario

Cover design by Leon Aureus
Type design by Blake Sproule

LIBRARY AND ARCHIVES CANADA CATALOGUING IN PUBLICATION

Moodie, Andrew, 1967-
Toronto the good / Andrew Moodie.

A play.
ISBN 978-0-88754-913-7

I. Title.

PS8576.O558T67 2010   C812'.54   C2009-907507-5

First edition: February 2010
Printed and bound in Canada by Canadian Printco, Scarborough

DEDICATED TO ARIANNA AND ZORA

PLAYERS' MANIFESTO (PART IV)

I

Science gives us intelligence. Art gives us wisdom.

Science gives us the ability to create a weapon that can destroy civilization.

Art gives us the wisdom to know that we should never use it.

II

Wisdom is shared through language.

A culture is a unit of collected wisdom.

There are unique cultures between languages.

There are unique cultures within one language.

III

There is only one theatre.

It has no colour. It has no race.

It has every colour. It has every race.

Theatres are united first by language.

Then by culture.

There are theatres that focus on one specific culture.

There are theatres that are open to all cultures.

Theatres that are culturally specific are necessary to collect the wisdom of a specific culture.

Theatres that are culturally open are necessary to share wisdom amongst all cultures.

It is important for theatres to exist that give a voice to specific cultures.

It is important for theatres to exist that embrace all cultures and share wisdom with everyone.

It is essential to the survival of our species on this planet that we share our wisdom with each other and future generations.

PLAYWRIGHT'S NOTES

I don't remember the moment I decided I wanted to write this play. I don't think there was one. My first produced play was *Riot*, and in the play the issue of gun violence and youth in Canada was explored. *Riot* was about being Canadian, not gun violence. But I suppose, lurking somewhere in that little nugget of my soul called the unconscious, the desire to say something about guns and youth and violence in Canada never left me.

I found myself reading newspaper articles. Then I found myself making notes. Then I was calling up people to talk to them about the issues. I spoke to people in education and in the legal system. I spoke to politicians and youth, troubled youth. I found myself going through the same process that I used to develop the script for *Riot*, I wrote down what people said and found a structured way to have what they said woven into a plot. I also did something I had never done before, I called a group of actors who I wanted to participate in the workshop and, before I wrote a word, I invited each of them out for lunch and asked them intimate details about their lives. I asked about their family history, how they came to Toronto, how they felt about the city and the issues. Then I carefully chose character names and created detailed character outlines. And then, when the fever was unbearable, I sat down and wrote the play.

It was like lancing a boil.

There are many people I must thank, and I will miss someone, but I should start with my wife, whom without her patience and understanding I would be nothing. I have to thank Ken Gass and everyone at Factory Theatre for their hard work, dedication, and belief in me. And I must thank the actors who participated in the original research and workshop: Amanda Parsons, Brian Marler, Louise Gauthier, Rhonda Roberts, Danny Waugh, and Ellie Downes.

And of course I must thank the actors who were in the final production: Stéphanie Broschart, Miranda Edwards, Sandra Forsell, Xuan Fraser, Brian Marler, Marcel Stewart, and the director, Phil Akin.

I had an interesting discussion with fellow actor Tony Nappo on Facebook about flashback monologues in the theatre. He made the argument that a playwright should never tell us about something that happens offstage, just show us, put the scene on the stage. It spawned a really interesting discussion that brought up some very valid points on all sides in a Facebook kind of way. I bring this up because I basically agree with Tony and I've taken great pains to make sure that most of the soliloquies deal with something that the character is experiencing in the moment.

If there's a moment when you're recounting something that happened offstage, make sure it's connected to what's happening to you right now, on stage before you. I want every moment you have on stage to be active, and I've worked really hard to that end, but at the same time, in life, people talk about things that happened "offstage" all the time. A moment ago, I went into the kitchen to grab a coffee where my wife was getting a snack ready for our daughters and she told me about a friend of hers whose daughter pooped in her pants in the schoolyard. If I were to write that scene I would have to decide, do I want the audience to see the kid crapping its pants, or do I want them to see my reaction to the story, followed by some disarmingly witty comment that sums up how we are all that little girl at least once in our life, etc.

I am also doing something that I've never done before. I am including my character name notes and character outlines. When choosing names for this play I wanted each of them to have some kind of significance. And as I mentioned above, for the main characters I wrote a page of character description. I am giving this to you so that if you, the actor, would like to use them, you can. If you don't want to, that's fine too.

I wrote the notes so that as I was writing I would always work towards each character having something about their nature that was incongruous in some way. Some of the notes I used, some I didn't. Some you may find helpful, some you may not. If you don't want to use them, if you want to come up with your own history, or even if you just don't believe in it, that's fine, but respect the actors that do. And if you're an actor who wants to use them, that's fine to and respect the ones that don't.

Pace: As with most of my plays, I want each of the actors to come in with their line, no pauses (unless absolutely necessary). I intend for the scenes to flow into each other, no blackouts, and no pauses in between.

Right before the intermission, the chorus names victims of gun violence. If you would like to replace a name with a more recent victim of gun violence, feel free.

And finally, I wrote this play to have immediacy, naturalness, sometimes even casualness, don't be afraid of it. I intend for you to bring yourself to the character and at times reveal a vulnerability to the audience.

Have fun, relax, and enjoy yourself.

CHARACTER NAMES

Below is a list of most of the characters in the play and a note about what the names mean. This is not a character description! I just thought you might like to know why I picked the name, and that's all.

THE ACCUSED: SOLOMON MOSEBY

Solomon Moseby was a black runaway slave who had stolen a horse in Kentucky to escape. When he arrived in Niagara, he was jailed, but the local black community surrounded the courthouse. Armed guards appeared who then shot into the crowd, resulting in the deaths of two black people, the arrest of twenty others and Moseby's escape. He later returned to the area.

THE SISTER OF THE ACCUSED: ROSE FORTUNE

Rose Fortune was the first female police officer in North America.

THE CROWN ATTORNEY: THOMAS MATTHEWS

In Thomas's star appearance in the New Testament, he doubts the resurrection of Jesus and demands to feel Jesus's wounds before being convinced.

In the Gospel of Matthew, Matthew is introduced as a tax collector.

THE CROWN ATTORNEY'S WIFE: ALMANDA MARCHAND

In 1914, at the start of World War I, volunteer Almanda Walker-Marchand wanted to raise funds to charter a hospital ship. So she organized an initial meeting of French-Canadian women in Ottawa. More than four hundred women answered her call and quickly grew into a formal association. In 1918 the Fédération nationale des femmes canadiennes-françaises was officially founded with Almanda as its first president.

THE DEFENCE ATTORNEY: SIMON PHILLIPS

Simon was a fisherman from Bethsaida. He is also referred to as Simon the Zealot.

In Phrygia, Philip preached with Bartholomew and, using the power of prayer, killed a large serpent in a temple devoted to serpent worship. They also healed many people who, obviously, suffered from snake bites. Philip was the apostle who was asked by Jesus what it would cost to buy bread for five thousand men.

THE DEFENCE ATTORNEY'S WIFE: FANNY ROSENFELD

Fanny "Bobbie" Rosenfeld, from Barrie, Ontario, was Canada's most famous female athlete of the first half of the twentieth century. She was a coach, sports official and administrator, and journalist.

THE DEFENCE ATTORNEY'S DAUGHTERS: REBECCA AND SARAH

Rebecca was the wife of Isaac and the mother of Jacob and Esau. Sarah was the wife of Abraham and the mother of Isaac.

THE POLICE OFFICER: ELSIE MacGILL

In America, the wartime role model was Rosie the Riveter. In Canada, it was Elsie MacGill, a war heroine who became known as the "Queen of the Hurricanes." In 1938, the thirty-five-year-old woman became chief aeronautical engineer at Canadian Car & Foundry.

THE REPORTER: MARY ANN SHADD

Mary Ann Shadd is acknowledged as the first black newspaper-woman in North America and the publisher of Canada's first anti-slavery newspaper.

THE WHITE STUDENT: ANN HARVEY

Ann Harvey "Grace Darling of Newfoundland," became famous for her bravery. When she was seventeen she helped rescue sixty-three shipwrecked sailors from the brig *Despatch* between the twelfth and fifteenth of July, 1828.

THE BLACK STUDENT: VIOLET PAULINE KING

Violet Pauline King is believed to be the first African-Canadian to practise law in 1954.

COMPETING WHITE ATTORNEY: PETER CASHIN

Major Peter John Cashin was a Newfoundland politician, businessman, and soldier.

IT GUY: WILLIAM WILLIS

The first black businessmen in Toronto were two contractors— Jack Mosee and William Willis. In 1799, they began the process of building a road from Yonge Street, York, westward through the Pinery.

FRIEND OF OFFICER MacGILL: CLARA BRETT MARTIN

Clara Brett Martin became the first female lawyer in the British Empire. She set up a law practice in Toronto.

SIMON'S ASSISTANT: THÉRÈSE CASGRAIN

Thérèse Casgrain—feminist reformer who was also the first woman in Quebec to lead a provincial political party.

"FRIEND" OF SIMON: ANGELIQUE

Marie-Joseph Angélique was a Portuguese-born black slave in Quebec who was tried and convicted of setting fire to her owner's home, burning much of what is now referred to as Old Montreal.

STRIPPER IN BAR: JENNIFER ALLAN

Jennifer Allan is a former sex worker who founded Jen's Kitchen, an outreach and food-relief service for women.

BARTENDER: JEFFREY REODICA

Jeffrey Reodica was part of a group of Filipino teenagers who were engaged in an altercation with a group of white teenagers on May 21, 2004. Plainclothes Toronto police officer Detective Constable Dan Belanger and his partner Detective Allen Love were in the process of arresting Reodica when Belanger shot him three times in the back. The teen died in hospital three days later.

TAXI DRIVER: GURDIT SINGH

Canadian Sikh leader Gurdit Singh challenged the "continuous passage" legislation. He hired a ship called the *Komagata Maru*, and planned a non-stop voyage to Vancouver with 376 East Indian immigrants. When the freighter anchored in Vancouver, Canadian immigration officials did not allow the men to disembark.

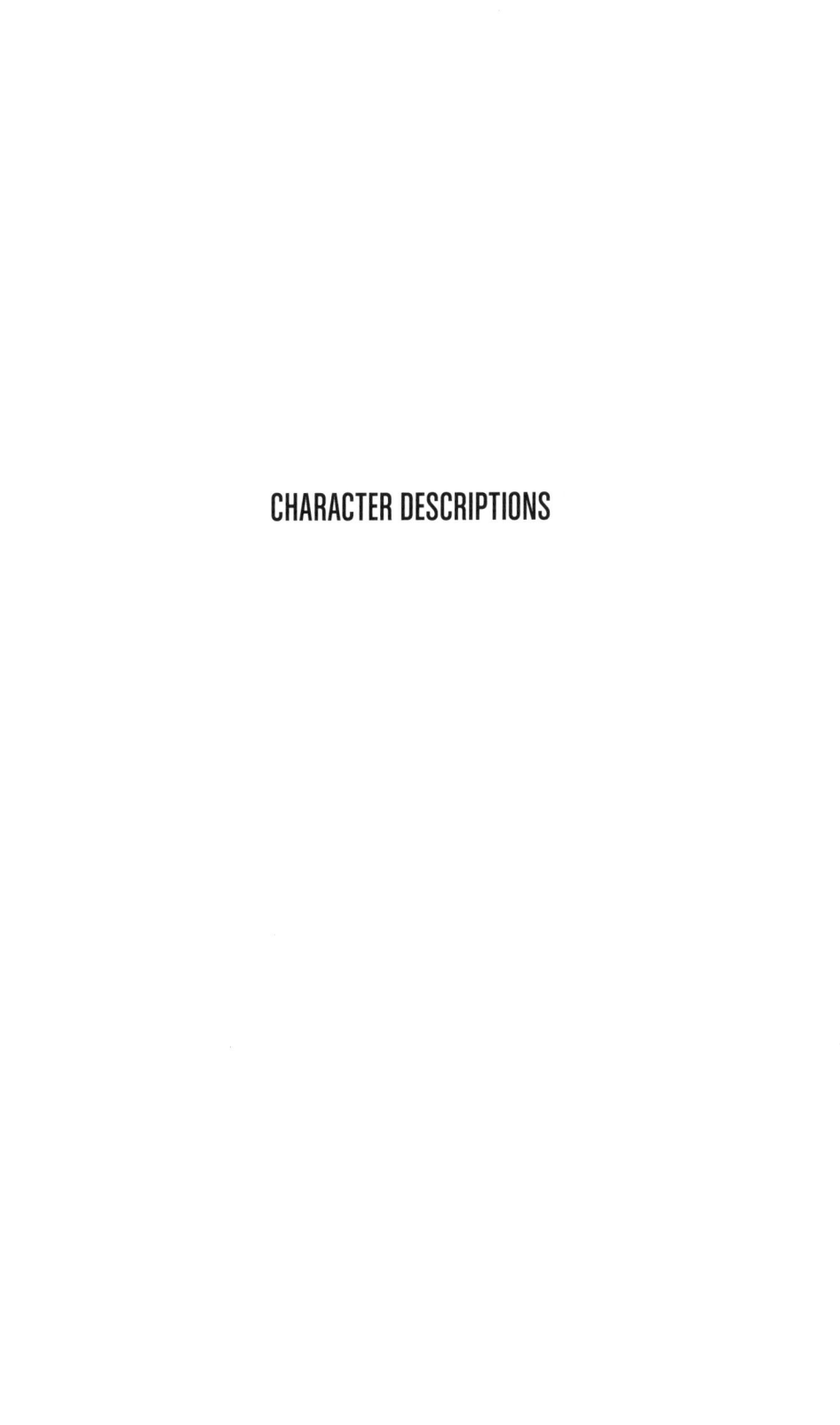

CHARACTER DESCRIPTIONS

THOMAS MATTHEWS

Place of Birth: Ottawa

Occupation: Crown attorney

Education: University of Ottawa

Father: Milton Matthews

Mother: Vanessa Matthews (née Keith)

Brothers / Sisters: Sandra, Katherine

Hobbies: Canadian history

Likes: The Ottawa Senators; pancakes; the smell of McDonald's french fries; Journey; ELO; Prince; Jimi Hendrix; jazz music; the Who; reggae music; Ayn Rand; Arthur Koestler; Karen Armstrong; Camille Paglia; James Baldwin; Wallace Thurman; *Star Wars* episodes 4, 5, 6; *Star Trek* (original series); Halle Berry; Lauren Graham; 1972 Ford Mustang; walking along the canal in Ottawa on a fall afternoon; dogs; Microsoft.

Dislikes: Rubbing dry fingers on dry paper; the Toronto Maple Leafs; President's Choice lasagna; rap music; 50 Cent; dancehall music; minivans; Noël Coward; Marshall McLuhan; Jacques Lacan; *Star Trek: The Next Generation*; *Star Wars* episodes 1, 2, 3; John Cusack; George Clooney; finding parking in Toronto; cats; Apple.

Physical Problems: Acid reflux, lower-back pain

Food Allergies: Apples

Phobias and Complexes: Mysophobia

Notes: Milton and Vanessa were both from Jamaica. They met in Toronto. Fell in love. They had their first child, Sandra, while living in Toronto. Then they moved to Kingston so that Milton could study at Queen's University, then they moved to Ottawa where Vanessa got a job managing the emergency room of the Civic Hospital and Milton was hired by the Department of Defence. There they had Thomas and Katherine.

Thomas dropped out of university for a year after an altercation with a professor about race. He returned to university after travelling through Spain, working for a jewellery-import company.

SIMON PHILLIPS

Place of Birth: Lethbridge, Alberta

Occupation: Defence Attorney

Education: University of British Columbia

Father: Jeremiah "Jerry" Abraham Phillips

Mother: Farahilde Phillips (née Gassinger)

Brothers / Sisters: Frank

Hobbies: Canadian history

Likes: *The Wire*; Stanley Kubrick; David Lynch; Woody Allen; reggae; Rush; Pink Floyd; Beastie Boys; Lil' Kim; Cormac McCarthy; Verner von Heidenstam; Charles Dickens; Albert Camus; the Edmonton Oilers; *Star Trek* (original series); *Star Wars* episodes 4, 5, 6; smoking; cats; Apple.

Dislikes: Canadian right-wing politics; American right-wing politics; the CBC; the Toronto Maple Leafs; *Star Trek: The Next*

Generation; *Star Wars* episodes 1, 2, 3; tequila; American cigarettes; Beck; the Smashing Pumpkins; Metallica; John Mayer; Mel Gibson; dogs; Microsoft.

Physical Problems: Colitis

Food Allergies: None

Phobias and Complexes: Aquaphobia

Notes: Jeremiah was an accountant that left a high-paying firm in Edmonton to work for First Nations municipal governments, working on their budgets and dealing with the federal government.

Farahilde wanted girls. She left nursing to become a stay-at-home mother who ran a daycare out of her home. Her father had died from cancer at a young age and her mother married a man who hated girls and always wanted a boy.

Jeremiah had to travel for many months, leaving Farahilde with the boys for long periods of time. She loved her sons but it was hard.

Simon learned to read in kindergarten. He skipped a grade. In university he discovered cocaine while working as a waiter. He started skipping classes.

Jeremiah died from a heart attack while Simon was in rehab.

Simon met his wife when he returned to university. She was studying acting. She left acting once they married.

Simon will never meet his wife's grandparents because his mother is Austrian and they are Holocaust survivors. He is not welcome at Passover. His wife's parents accept him. Mostly.

ALMANDA MATTHEWS

Place of Birth: Ottawa, Ontario

Occupation: High-school teacher

Education: University of Ottawa

Father: Sebastian Marchand

Mother: Celeste Marchand (née Lefebvre)

Brothers / Sisters: Christophe, Natalie, Marie-Josée, Pierre, Renée, Jean

Hobbies: Knitting

Likes: Reading, *La vie, la vie*, John Cusack movies, vacationing in Jamaica, *Tetris*, Jean LeLoup, Genesis (the band), curried chicken roti, patties, reggae, leather, dancing, President's Choice lasagna baked in the oven.

Dislikes: René Simard, McDonald's food, CHEZ 106 (Ottawa radio station), Toronto, tourtière, David Letterman, Pierre Trudeau, big-budget Hollywood movies, sitcoms, Alberta, President's Choice lasagna baked in the microwave.

Physical Problems: Lower-back pain, swollen feet

Food Allergies: None

Phobias and Complexes: Claustrophobia

Notes: Almanda's father worked in the office of the prime minister from 1969 to 1984.

Almanda's mother stayed at home. She died from breast cancer three years ago.

Grew up in the east end of Ottawa.

Almanda met Thomas during at a University of Ottawa fundraiser for cystic fibrosis. Carleton University had dropped their cystic fibrosis fundraiser because it wasn't "inclusive" enough. Almanda discovered Thomas and debated what that meant all night.

Suffered from bulimia as a teenager.

Almanda used to date a Québécois hockey player who used to play for the New York Islanders.

ELSIE MacGILL

Place of Birth: Halifax, Nova Scotia

Occupation: Police officer

Education: Saint Mary's University, Political Science

Father: Earnest MacGill

Mother: Margot MacGill (née Vikaras)

Brothers / Sisters: Roderick

Hobbies: Hockey, collecting Barbie paraphernalia

Likes: Don Cherry, the Toronto Maple Leafs, CFL football, alphabet soup, Facebook, Lithuanian food, velvet, Jimi Hendrix, *Family Guy*, Kurt Vonnegut, wine, monster trucks.

Dislikes: Ron MacLean, green-pea soup, *World of Warcraft*, horror movies, tap water, Will Ferrell, Pet Shop Boys, processed cheese.

Physical Problems: Severe dermatitis on left elbow

Food Allergies: Garlic

Phobias and Complexes: Elevators

Notes: Earnest was a family doctor, Margot was a chef at a Lithuanian restaurant. Mother died of a heart attack at the restaurant. After that, Earnest became obsessed with his daughter's eating habits for the rest of her life.

Father has recently retired and has multiple sclerosis. He moved to Toronto so that Elsie could take care of him.

Roderick, Elsie's brother, lives in Phoenix, Arizona, and writes for a weekly alternative newspaper and a music blog.

Elsie recently separated from a partner of five years who had become an alcoholic.

Elsie won a public-speaking award in the tenth grade. Two days before her mother died.

Father was diagnosed with MS three years ago.

SOLOMON MOSEBY

Place of Birth: Kingston, Jamaica

Occupation: Unemployed

Education: Bloor Collegiate Institute

Father: Unknown

Mother: Deisha Moseby

Brothers / Sisters: Rose Fortune

Hobbies: PS3

Likes: *Call of Duty*, rap, hip hop, pot, hot dogs, Jackie Chan, Ray Bradbury.

Dislikes: Homosexuals, ice cream, the world.

Physical Problems: Impacted wisdom tooth

Food Allergies: None

Phobias and Complexes: Cats

Notes: Mother left Jamaica to work as a maid. Rose and Solomon lived with their aunt in a fancy house in Kingston. Aunt hated them.

When Rose and Solomon came to Canada, they loved the snow, at first.

Mother died of AIDS when Solomon turned thirteen.

Solomon dropped out of high school at the age of fifteen.

He once told his sister that he was going to make a movie based on Bradbury's "A Sound of Thunder." She laughed at him.

ROSE FORTUNE MOSEBY

Place of Birth: Kingston, Jamaica

Occupation: Chambermaid

Education: Bloor Collegiate Institute

Father: Unknown

Mother: Deisha Moseby

Brothers / Sisters: Solomon

Hobbies: Sudoku

Likes: Soap operas, curried goat, dance halls, Céline Dion, Facebook games, anime, fancy soaps, the beach, hard dough bread, ginger beer, plantains, rice and peas, Christianity.

Dislikes: Chocolate, flowers, gold teeth, dogs, ackee, drugs, tomatoes, curried goat, roti, willow trees, politics, violent movies, Walt Disney movies, computers, snow.

Physical Problems: Diabetes, allergic to pollen

Food Allergies: Lactose intolerant

Phobias and Complexes: Flying

Notes: Mother left Jamaica to work as a maid. Rose and Solomon lived with their aunt in a fancy house in Kingston. Aunt hated them.

When Rose and Solomon came to Canada, they loved the snow, at first.

Mother died of AIDS when Rose turned sixteen.

Rose got a job at the Four Seasons hotel chain and raised her brother by herself.

PRODUCTION INFORMATION

Toronto the Good was first produced by Factory Theatre, Toronto, Ontario, from January 31–March 1, 2009, with the following company:

Stéphanie Broschart	Actor 3
Miranda Edwards	Actor 5
Sandra Forsell	Actor 4
Xuan Fraser	Actor 1
Brian Marler	Actor 2
Marcel Stewart	Actor 6

Directed by Philip Akin
Set and costumes by Kelly Wolf
Lighting design by Rebecca Picherak
Sound design by Christopher Stanton
Stage management by Andrea Schurman

Actor 1: Thomas Matthews, Chorus 6, Jeffrey Reodica

Actor 2: Officer A, Simon Phillips, Peter Cashin, Chorus 3

Actor 3: Almanda Marchand, Chorus 5, Sarah, CFRB Host 2

Actor 4: Officer Elsie MacGill, Ann Harvey, Chorus 4, Rebecca, Jennifer, CFRB Host 1

Actor 5: Violet, Chorus 2, Mary Ann Shadd, Rose Fortune Moseby, Angelique

Actor 6: Chorus 1, William Willis, Solomon Moseby, Gurdit Singh, Young Male

TORONTO THE GOOD

ACT ONE

Lights up on THOMAS, *sitting centre stage.*

THOMAS   So the thing is, I'm in my shorts, and not like my funky, overpriced, Little Star Bermudas. I'm like in the black Adidas with the white stripes down the side. My T-shirt's got the whole *Cool Runnings* Jamaican flag on the back, 'cause my mom got it for me last time she went to visit Uncle Bob.

Lights up on bike.

I've been painting and tearing up drywall all day, and all I want is some popcorn. That's all I want. I've got a six of Stella in the fridge getting nice and frosty. My wife's got the DVD of some light Hollywood fare, I don't even remember what it was. I think... I think it was some John Cusak thing 'cause she's got the biggest hard-on for that guy, but that's okay.

He is now at the bike. Maybe he sits on it, maybe he rides it, maybe he touches it, maybe he just looks at it.

	So. Popcorn. That's all I want. And I'm on my wife's bike, 'cause the chain on my bike is rusty, and I keep saying I'm gonna fix it and get back into the same shape I was in when I was twenty-seven, blah blah blah. I'm halfway back home and out of nowhere I hear that short siren blast and the flash of red and blue.
OFFICER A	Stop right there please.
THOMAS	Uh... sure. Yeah. Okay.
	OFFICER A looks at THOMAS with flashlight.
OFFICER A	Where are you coming from?
THOMAS	And I'm actually thinking, oh my God, I wonder what's wrong. Is my wife okay? That's where I go. My mind is racing forward, I'm thinking there was a home invasion, my wife's in hospital, they've been searching the streets for me...
OFFICER A	Sir, where are you coming from?
THOMAS	Oh, uh, the store, I just.... Is everything all right?
OFFICER A	And where are you going?
THOMAS	I'm going home. Is everything...
OFFICER A	You live in this neighbourhood?
THOMAS	And then I'm slowly starting to clue in.
OFFICER A	Sir, answer the question, you live in this neighbourhood?

THOMAS	And it's not the first time this has happened to me.
OFFICER A	Sir...
THOMAS	The very first time I was on a date... I was with the woman who would eventually become my wife.

ALMANDA enters.

	We were still living in Ottawa, walking through Confederation Park and this cruiser speeds onto the grass...
ALMANDA	Maudit sacrament!
THOMAS	She's all over it.
ALMANDA	La seul calice de raison que vous êtes icite, c'est parce qu'y est noire!
OFFICER A	Sir.
ALMANDA	Tabarnak calice!
OFFICER A	Answer the question. Do you live in this...
THOMAS	Uh... yeah. I live just over there.
OFFICER A	You got any ID?
THOMAS	I uh... I don't have my wallet on me, I've got it at home, just hold on a sec...

THOMAS walks towards the house.

OFFICER A	Don't move! Stay right there, do not move!

	Do you understand me?
THOMAS	And then I clue in to the fact that this guy is scared. He's scared of me. And I get… it's like… I want him to stay cool, so I get really cool.
OFFICER A	What's your name?
THOMAS	Thomas Matthews, I live at 135 Delaware, just over there. If you wanna come with me, I can…
OFFICER A	Stay right there and don't move.

OFFICER moves away from THOMAS.

| THOMAS | And then the incredulity starts to spark and becomes a kind of smouldering rage that… actually, well… there are two things happening at the same time: the rage and the fear. The fear that your rage is going to get out of control and make the situation worse. |

The OFFICER returns with a ticket.

OFFICER A	Get a bike light.
THOMAS	What?
OFFICER A	Get a bike light.

The OFFICER leaves.

| ALMANDA | Where the hell were you? |
| THOMAS | I'm still in shock. And I think about not telling her, 'cause I know how she's going to react. |

ALMANDA looks at the ticket.

ALMANDA   I mean, what, a human being can't go to the damn store without...

THOMAS   And I'm not sure if I want to be comforted, or if I just want to bitch about it, or if I want to be left alone...

ALMANDA   We live in a police state! I mean, can't a...

THOMAS   So I tell her I'd rather just watch the movie and forget about it.

ALMANDA   You sure?

THOMAS   And I have no idea what... *The Ice Harvest.* Billy Bob Thornton, John Cusack. Both acting their little hearts out. I don't remember a thing.

OFFICER MacGILL enters in uniform. AL-MANDA leaves.

OFFICER MacGILL   What was that?

THOMAS   After the fourth Stella, I can fall asleep without too much trouble.

OFFICER MacGILL sitting. Lights change.

OFFICER MacGILL   Sorry, I missed that?

THOMAS   Don't be sorry, I was mumbling. I was just asking if you were hungry.

OFFICER MacGILL   Not really.

THOMAS	It's lunch. We don't have to do this here. There's a food court down...
OFFICER MacGILL	Actually, I'm really embarrassed about this, but I'm doing the Zone.
THOMAS	The Zone?
OFFICER MacGILL	Yeah, it's this thing where they send you food. They mail it to you...
THOMAS	Someone mails you food...
OFFICER MacGILL	Yeah, and you have to eat at very specific times, and I've already had my Zone, and I can't eat for another hour and a half and I'm very embarrassed so don't ask me about it.
THOMAS	I'll leave you alone.
OFFICER MacGILL	Thanks.
THOMAS	Nervous?
OFFICER MacGILL	Nope.
THOMAS	Really?
OFFICER MacGILL	Should I be?
THOMAS	Not at all. Not at all. Now has anyone explained to you what a charter motion is?
OFFICER MacGILL	No.
THOMAS	Okay. The defendant, one Solomon Moseby, is accusing you of racial discrimination contrary to section 4 of the Human Rights,

	Citizenship and Multiculturalism Act.
OFFICER MacGILL	And that means…
THOMAS	It means that the defence lawyer is desperate. So. I'm going to prep you for cross-examination. And… this isn't the fun part.
OFFICER MacGILL	There's a fun part?
THOMAS	I'm gonna pretend to be the defence attorney, and I'll have to really dig in there, get some nitty-gritty details. The key to all this is relax. Tell the truth. Don't get angry. You can tell me anything. Nothing's going to happen to you. Okay?
OFFICER MacGILL	I'm ready.
THOMAS	It says here in your testimony that you observed the defendant, a young, black male, in his vehicle, driving erratically.
OFFICER MacGILL	That is correct.
THOMAS	Richmond and Peter.
OFFICER MacGILL	Yes.
THOMAS	How exactly was he driving erratically?
OFFICER MacGILL	He was driving north on Peter. Made a fairly wide left onto Richmond. As he corrected, he fishtailed a bit. Came to a sudden stop about a metre and a half away from the curb and then reversed suddenly into a parking position.
THOMAS	And you were…

OFFICER MacGILL	I was parked just west of Widmer.
THOMAS	Were the roads icy?
OFFICER MacGILL	There was a bit of hard snow, and ice. Mostly dry road though.
THOMAS	So the car fishtailed a bit. So what?
OFFICER MacGILL	Uh...
THOMAS	What made you... what gave you concern.
OFFICER MacGILL	It was 4:40 in the morning. The clubs had been closed for a while...
THOMAS	This was a Wednesday?
OFFICER MacGILL	Thursday morning.
THOMAS	Right.
OFFICER MacGILL	My first thought was DUI.
THOMAS	So you approach the vehicle.
OFFICER MacGILL	That's right.
THOMAS	Alone.
OFFICER MacGILL	What's that?
THOMAS	You were alone.
OFFICER MacGILL	Yes.
THOMAS	You're the only witness.

OFFICER MacGILL	Yes, that's right.
THOMAS	Well, that's convenient.
OFFICER MacGILL	I beg your pardon?
THOMAS	You approach the vehicle.
OFFICER MacGILL	Yes.
THOMAS	What happens next?
OFFICER MacGILL	I, uh…
THOMAS	Okay okay okay okay, look, the defence attorney is going to go at you way… much tougher than I am right now, and you're going to have to answer with yes or no right away.
OFFICER MacGILL	Right.
THOMAS	If you need to think about the answer, take the time you need, but no stuttering. At all.
OFFICER MacGILL	Okay.
THOMAS	And he's gonna throw in a lot of snarky little remarks in there too. Let it all roll of your back.
OFFICER MacGILL	Got it.
THOMAS	Before we go to trial, I'll give you a real… we'll do a complete rehearsal, where I'm just gonna hammer you hard, but I'm doing this now to just… put it in your head, calm, collected, cool.

OFFICER MacGILL	I got it. Try me again.
THOMAS	Very good. Now. At what point did you notice the defendant was black?
OFFICER MacGILL	I didn't.
THOMAS	Okay, you can't... uh...
OFFICER MacGILL	I didn't.
THOMAS	Okay, the windows of the car were not tinted. The area is well lit...
OFFICER MacGILL	I didn't notice he was black. I didn't.
THOMAS	Okay, but... okay. If you're on... what was it? Richmond. Facing west...
OFFICER MacGILL	I swear to you I didn't notice he was black.
THOMAS	Okay, yeah, but if you're just west of Widmer, you're right at the intersection. So you're gonna see the driver...
OFFICER MacGILL	When he got to the light I wasn't paying attention to him. I was looking down at the computer, the car was in my periphery, as the car goes into the turn and starts to fishtail, I look up, I see the back of his head in a darkened car. After I pull up behind him and I'm walking to the car, sure, yeah, I notice he's black.
THOMAS	Keep it calm.
OFFICER MacGILL	It's just... I know that the race thing is at play in all of this and...

THOMAS	Breathe. Remember, I'm not here to judge you. You can tell me anything. Remember?
OFFICER MacGILL	Yeah.
THOMAS	Now, you pull up behind him. Park on the side of the road?
OFFICER MacGILL	Uh…
THOMAS	Don't do that.
OFFICER MacGILL	Damn! Right. Right.
THOMAS	Did you park on the side of the road?
OFFICER MacGILL	Yes.
THOMAS	And so you get to the defendant's car and…
OFFICER MacGILL	Can I say something?
THOMAS	Can we finish this first?
OFFICER MacGILL	I would really like to say something right now it I could.
THOMAS	You want to tell me that you're not a racist person. Trust me, Officer MacGill, I think you are an incredible officer. I have a lot of respect for you…
OFFICER MacGILL	Don't blow smoke up my ass. Please.
THOMAS	THEY want to make this about race. Let them try. The more calm you are…

MacGILL tries to interject.

	Bahp, ah, let me finish. The more calm you are...
OFFICER MacGILL	Please, can I just...
THOMAS	The more direct and matter-of-fact you are...
OFFICER MacGILL	Listen! Where I grew up... the high school I went to in Halifax, black kids go in the north door, white kids go in the south door. I get to go in the north door because my dad is one of the few doctors who'll take in black patients.
THOMAS	Officer MacGill...
OFFICER MacGILL	I don't see colour. I don't.
THOMAS	Officer MacGill...
OFFICER MacGILL	And it just pisses me off because...
THOMAS	Officer MacGill, you cannot get emotional on the stand. You can't. You can say the exact same thing, but... as a matter of fact, what we're going to do is this. Tonight, I want you to write down exactly what you just told me, and then we are going to pare it down to a couple of sentences, a paragraph maybe, and then that is what you can say on the stand. Okay?
OFFICER MacGILL	I just want you to... I needed to get that off my chest 'cause...
THOMAS	No, hey. This is a tough process. And uh... I understand. Now, let's start again.

ALMANDA *enters.* THOMAS *and* OFFICER
MACGILL *exit.*

ALMANDA   And I miss the damn streetcar!? Come ON!
It's not supposed to leave for another... ah!
Whew! Need to just... breathe for a second.
Let it go. Let it all go. Ah, my feet. I shouldn't
have run. There's supposed to be a streetcar
at a quarter past. I search in my bag for the
book I'm reading. It's called *Y'a des moments
si merveilleux* and you've never heard of it.
It's by Dominique Michel, and you've never
heard of her, and I'm too embarrassed to tell
you anything about it, you just have to know
it's an escape. That's all. It's an escape from
the vomiting and the...

ANN *and* VIOLET *enter.* ANN *shouts from
across the stage.*

ANN   Hey, miss, ya want a lift?

ALMANDA   Ha ha, very funny.

ANN   Seriously, we're gonna hit a tattoo parlour,
get the Britney special.

ALMANDA   Violet.

VIOLET   What?

ALMANDA   I didn't see you in class today.

VIOLET   I had my period.

ALMANDA   Yeah yeah, listen, don't miss another class, I
don't want to have to fail you.

VIOLET	Whatevah.
ALMANDA	Ann, could you give Violet the assignment please?
ANN	Think your streetcar's here, Mrs. M.
ALMANDA	Give her the assignment, Ann!
ANN	Will do, Mrs. M.

ANN and VIOLET exit.

ALMANDA	And I'm on the streetcar. Where's the damn token? I can't find it, so I have to put in... what is it now... how much?! You've got to be joking, when did that happen? And the people behind me are pushing past me 'cause they're tired of waiting. And the doors slam shut and...

OFFICER MacGILL enters on her cellphone.

OFFICER MacGILL	I'm at Yonge and College headed south. And... *(to the phone)* Pick up, pick up the phone. What should I do. Head down to Dundas. Waltz around Eaton's. Window shop. I could go into work but by the time I get there... *(leaving a message)* Hey Dad, it's me. Uh... just wanted to know if you wanted me to grab anything on the way home. I'm not at work. It was... the whole thing went... I'll tell ya later. Call my cell, okay? *(She hangs up.)* I don't want to go in. Back to that... desk. Not right now. I want to... what do I want to do? I wander into the magazine store on the northeast corner of College. Lookin around at magazines. 'Nother fucking story about Tom

fucking Cruise. I leave. I'm standing on the sidewalk. What was I thinking! "I don't see colour." What a stupid thing to say. Dammit! I'm... I just wanted him to... get me. I just...

Looks at phone.

I'll go down to Yonge and Dundas, walk around. *(She starts to dial her father's number again.)* Check out HMV. Then I'll head into work. That'll do. Yeah. I start...

Lights change.

THOMAS   Running around the kitchen like a madman, trying to get dinner ready so that when she gets in the door she can just sit down and eat. I've got a President's Choice Chicken Wellington in the oven. It'll probably be ready about ten minutes after she arrives. And I'm barely paying attention to what I'm doing because before I came home, I sat in my car, right about where Officer MacGill said she was, and I'm thinking, it's not really that hard to see the driver of the car, and I know it was dark, but how dark could it actually be? And I realize that...

ALMANDA arrives home.

ALMANDA   Hey honey.

THOMAS   Hey my beautiful, beautiful, mother of my offspring.

They kiss.

ALMANDA   You forgot the coleslaw.

THOMAS	I remembered the coleslaw, but it's going to take another ten, fifteen to get everything on the table.
ALMANDA	Did you remember the licence sticker?
THOMAS	Ah…
ALMANDA	I need the car!
THOMAS	You can drive the car.
ALMANDA	I'm not getting stopped by the police again. I'm not.
THOMAS	I can get the ticket taken care of. It's not a problem. Drive the car.
ALMANDA	Give me the application, I'll do it myself.
THOMAS	I thought you said you couldn't get the time off work to go in.
ALMANDA	I know, I don't care, I just want to get it done.
THOMAS	Then use my car.
ALMANDA	I don't drive standard.
THOMAS	Give me forty-five minutes, I can teach you how…
ALMANDA	I'm not driving your car, and I'm not taking a taxi! Just give me the damn application so we can be done with this. Please.
THOMAS	I can do it. I will do it. Tomorrow. I'm sorry, I'll remember. I promise.

ALMANDA	You keep saying that.
	ALMANDA goes to the phone to check voice mail.
THOMAS	I will, I'll get it. Come. Sit down. Tell me about your day.
ALMANDA	Uh... so remember I was saying how the board was—oh, you've got a message from a someone at the *Toronto Star*...
THOMAS	I got that one. Thanks.
	There are no new messages.
ALMANDA	So the board was going on and on about how the new Dell computers are such a great deal, and...
THOMAS	Food's ready.
ALMANDA	So the board releases the audit and now there's this whole TDSB investigation happening...
THOMAS	It's gonna get ugly, isn't it.
ALMANDA	And I'm gonna love every second of it. How's the case?
THOMAS	It's funny, you know, I uh... I want to talk to the kid.
ALMANDA	You want to talk to him?
THOMAS	Yeah.
ALMANDA	And what do you want to say?

THOMAS	I uh... I don't know. I guess I... want to say the magic words that will make him change his life around and all that Walt Disney crap... I don't know.
ALMANDA	Then talk to him.
THOMAS	I can't.
ALMANDA	Why not?
THOMAS	I'm not allowed.
ALMANDA	Why not?
THOMAS	I'm not allowed. Any word on the maternity leave issues?
ALMANDA	Honey?
THOMAS	Yes.
ALMANDA	How would you feel if...
THOMAS	Yes...
ALMANDA	Maybe if I didn't go back to work.
THOMAS	After your maternity leave?
ALMANDA	For a while. After. Yeah.
THOMAS	We kind of budgeted for both of us to...
ALMANDA	I know...
THOMAS	I mean we agreed that we need two incomes.

ALMANDA	I know, and I know I said I wouldn't do this, but... the thought's been just... it's been floating around in my head there for a while. Not, like... a while, but...
THOMAS	The mortgage payments are...
ALMANDA	We could move.
THOMAS	We could move?
ALMANDA	We don't have to live here, we could move.
THOMAS	Where?
ALMANDA	There's a place in the Glebe...
THOMAS	I'm not moving back to Ottawa.
ALMANDA	Two storeys. Large kitchen. A yard.
THOMAS	I'm not moving back to Ottawa.
ALMANDA	It's two forty-nine, nine.
THOMAS	Two forty-nine, nine. In the Glebe?
ALMANDA	Walking distance from the canal. It's kind of small, but...
THOMAS	That's pretty amazing for the Glebe.
ALMANDA	I've got a link to it on MLS. You can just take a look at it just for fun.
THOMAS	You're the one that got us here in the first place.

ALMANDA	I know, I know.
THOMAS	Two forty-nine, nine. Huhn.
	They turn out to the audience.
ALMANDA	And so we eat.
THOMAS	I eat. She takes two bites of the coleslaw and vomits.
ALMANDA	Then we sit on the couch and watch some insipid reality TV.
THOMAS	You watch the TV, I sit with my laptop...
ALMANDA	I hate when he does that.
THOMAS	Just checking out the scores. News sites.
ALMANDA	Until I put my feet on your legs, pushing the laptop away.
THOMAS	And I think about my fears.
ALMANDA	And I worry about the future.
THOMAS	And then I'm turning off the lights.
ALMANDA	And we're in bed.
	Lights down on ALMANDA and THOMAS, lights up on SIMON. REBECCA and SARAH speak from off stage.
SIMON	And then I'm up to the sound of a screaming child. It's seven twenty and I've slept through my alarm. That's great, that's just

great. If I don't shower at six a.m. sharp... ah! I hate this! I grab the one-year-old out of the crib and grab a diaper. The three-year-old is still sleeping. Miraculously. Excellent. I can change the one-year-old's diaper downstairs, plunk a *Baby Einstein* into the old DVD player and buy myself ten minutes to throw breakfast together. I start peeling a banana and the one-year-old starts screaming for her sippy cup. Two points to me for filling the sippy cups last night and putting them in the fridge. I open the cupboard and we're out of bread. Oh for fff... Pete's sake! I was going to throw some jam on a piece of bread with some sliced banana, but that plan goes out the window, and now the three-year-old's up and is screaming for me to...

REBECCA   Daddy! Carry me down the stairs!

SIMON   And in my calmest Daddy voice, I say, "I can't carry you down the stairs, walk down the stairs and go pee, we're going to have breakfast in two minutes, okay."

REBECCA   I want you to carry me!!!

SIMON   Rebecca, come downstairs, go to the washroom now. I'm not asking you again.

REBECCA   Daddyyyyy!

SIMON   I've got two minutes. Where the hell are the Farley biscuits. I swear my wife hides them because she hates them. I know she hates them... ahah! One. One Farley biscuit. Okay, that goes to Sarah. Milk in a bowl, microwave, spoon, you're done. Now, Rebecca.

Banana, orange, cheese. It's not an award-winning breakfast, but she will eat it. Now, how the hell am I going to shower? My wife is with her family in Buffalo, I've got twenty minutes before I have to get them to daycare. You're not supposed to shower while the kids are eating because they could choke and die. But can I go to this meeting this morning without a shower? Well, Sarah's in the high chair, strapped in. Rebecca is old enough to tell me if something's wrong, I'll put on Treehouse, she'll be good. They'll be good. They will. I'm doing it. I hop in the shower. Bathroom door wide open, I yell down to Rebecca every couple of minutes, "How's it going down there!"

REBECCA   Dad, I'm watching my show!

SIMON   And I'm out of the shower, shaving like a madman, thinking, "Single mothers should be given a freaking medal of honour." So I've got the kids' clothes, Sarah has decided she doesn't want to wear clothing today.

SARAH   Naaaaa!

SIMON   They're dressed, we're out the door, I look at the time and if I don't hurry I'm going to be late, and the Crown attorney is going to think this is some kind of power play, but it's not, and I'm wondering how to handle it. I could lie, I could tell him the car broke down. I could tell him...

REBECCA   I love you, Daddy.

SIMON	I love you too, honey. Don't forget your lunch! And I'm racing along Mortimer to take Pottery Road to Bayview and that gets me right downtown in seven minutes flat. If I'm late, he's gonna be pissed but I don't know how much I care. The charges are a load of crap. Waste of my friggin time. Oops, traffic cop with radar. Got to slow down, got to slow down, got to…

THOMAS in an office. Reading a book. Looks at his watch.

THOMAS	This is some kind of power play. I hate that. It's so high school. I go back to my book. It's about the history of…

SIMON enters.

SIMON	Sorry I'm late. I got a late start getting the kids off to daycare, and one thing snowballs into another.
THOMAS	Don't worry about it.
SIMON	I'm serious, really sorry about this, I'll make it up to you
THOMAS	Hey, listen, I'm… my wife's going in for the ultrasound right when we get the charter motion, so…
SIMON	Congratulations!
THOMAS	Thanks.
SIMON	First one?

THOMAS	First one.
SIMON	Hhhh. I missed the first ultrasound too, I beat myself up about it so bad, but I'll tell ya, the second ultrasound. That's the real show. You want a boy or a girl?
THOMAS	Anything.

SIMON takes out a small notepad. Writes on it.

| SIMON | You're gonna go out, you're gonna buy these shoes, they're called Robeez. Buy a ton of them. And get your pediatrician NOW. |

SIMON gives note to THOMAS.

THOMAS	You've got to be kidding me.
SIMON	I am dead serious. Call today. This city is flippin pediatrician dry.
THOMAS	I'll remember that. Thanks.
SIMON	And say goodbye to a good night's sleep.
THOMAS	I'm ready.
SIMON	No you're not. Trust me. The first few days, you think, "I can handle this." Then week after day after... last night, my three-year-old is just screaming her head off at three a.m., and I'm thinking, "Didn't the UN declare sleep deprivation a form of torture? Is there any way I can bring my children up in front of the World Court?" Then they go and do something adorable, and.... Okay, quick story, then

I'm done. Just last month our cat died, and it's still... I still get a little choked up. It was leukemia. It was freaking awful. So my eldest overhears us talking to the vet, and she says, "Daddy, what does dying mean?" And I'm already a little touchy and I have no idea what to say, and so I go, "Well, what do you think it means, honey?" She thinks, and I can see the idea come to her, and calmly she says, "It's when you get smaller and smaller and smaller and then you're free."

THOMAS   Wow.

SIMON   Hahn?

THOMAS   That's something.

SIMON   She's a genius. She's a freaking poet. She's gonna win the Giller Prize at fourteen.

THOMAS   Sounds like it to me.

SIMON   Okay, let's get to work. I apologize, when I hear someone's having a kid I come off as sounding like I know everything. Just tell me to shut up any time you like.

THOMAS   No no. It's...

SIMON   So let's get to it. What are you offering?

THOMAS   Six years.

SIMON   Oh you've got to be kidding me!!!

THOMAS   The Attorney General is taking a hard stance on...

SIMON	Drop the weapons charges. Write him a ticket. That's a gift.
THOMAS	Six years.
	SIMON trying to figure it out.
SIMON	Okay, so you are so incredibly afraid our motion is going to go through that you're trying to get me to take half that, just to get your conviction.
THOMAS	On the contrary, we are so confident of our victory, we think you should know we're going for the full sentence. If you'd like to settle this right now, I'd take five and a half, but that's as low as I'd go.
SIMON	So your cop...
THOMAS	Officer MacGill.
SIMON	She just happened to see my client driving erratically, and just so happened to inspect the car, and just so happened to find a gun.
THOMAS	You read the report.
SIMON	I want you to listen very carefully to everything I'm about to say. My client was racially profiled. There was no swerving, there was no erratic behaviour. Officer MacGill is lying.
THOMAS	Is she?
SIMON	Officer MacGill saw a black person in a car. She stopped him because he's black. Because

the Toronto Police Services is a racist, bigoted, oppressive organization.

THOMAS   That so?

SIMON   Hey, Sherlock, get on the Internet, go to Wikipedia...

THOMAS   Wikipedia.

SIMON   Read their history.

THOMAS   Sure.

SIMON   And is Bill Blair, our chief of police, is he going to do anything about it? No, he's not. And you know why?

THOMAS   Let me guess...

SIMON   His job is to pat the cops on the back, tell the media whatever the hell they want to hear, and stay in the job long enough to collect a big, fat, freaking pension!

THOMAS   You obviously feel very passionately about your position.

SIMON   My client's charter rights have been VIOLATED! I mean come ON! How can... okay. You may not understand this concept, but I'll try and spell it out for you: every human being should be treated equally.

THOMAS   I understand the concept.

SIMON   Rich, poor, any colour, any religion, any orientation...

THOMAS	I know.
SIMON	Now, of course, it was easier to treat the poor with respect when they were all Irish, and Portuguese, and Italian. But somewhere along the way, the poor got darker, and...
THOMAS	And the police are used by the white, oppressive, military-industrial complex to suppress the poor, cowering, dark-skinned underclass. Simon, I gotta tell ya, this is nothing new to me. I have spent many a night, many a night, staying up late, drinking a lot of Scotch, and tearing down the white man. And I enjoyed it. I still enjoy it on occasion.

THOMAS gets ready to leave.

SIMON	Drop the weapons charges.
THOMAS	But that was a different time. It was a different place. It really was. That place is gone now.
SIMON	Tom. Drop the weapons charges.
THOMAS	Gun violence is a very serious problem.
SIMON	Tom...
THOMAS	It's a top priority for Bill Blair, the mayor, the premier, and the prime minister.
SIMON	Drop the weapons charges, give the kid a traffic ticket, and we're out of here.
THOMAS	And it's a top priority for me. My name is Thomas, not Tom. Tell your client six years.

And never, ever, lecture me about race, or morality, or human rights ever again. Get me, Sherlock?

SIMON   Don't let the door hit your ass on the way out!

THOMAS   Fuck you.

THOMAS leaves.

CHORUS 1, 2, and 4 enter with a basketball.

CHORUS 1/2/4   Aaaaaand break!

CHORUS 1, 2, and 4 toss a basketball to each other as they recite poetry.

CHORUS 2   Palm trees and rainy summers.

ALMANDA   I've got forty minutes while Principal Freedman has an assembly on Choices.

CHORUS 4   Sweaty days of nothing at all.

ALMANDA   I'm doing my best to get a vanilla yogourt down my throat, and going over...

She burps, might vomit.

Désolé. I gave the kids a poetry assignment.

CHORUS 1   When I moved to Canada, I was quite a little girl.

ALMANDA   It's the first time I've done this and I don't know if it's gonna work.

CHORUS 2   Didn't know much but I wanted to grow

ALMANDA	Before I hit them with Robert Service and T.S. Eliot, I want to get them thinking like poets.
CHORUS 4	I was always in the dark, trying to hide Then I wonder why I am so shy.
ALMANDA	Some of it's not bad. Some of it has that…
CHORUS 1	I wish I could cry loud enough for you to know how flooded my heart is. From the tears of your silence that is louder than anything in the world.
ALMANDA	It's… young. You know. It's just young. That's fine. And then some of it…
CHORUS 2	Basketball is my favourite sport I like the way it dribbles Up and down the court

CHORUS 1 and 2 leave. CHORUS 4 becomes ANN and hovers at the edge of the scene.

ALMANDA	Yeah, well. The important thing is that they really start to look at the world. That they try to see the layers of meaning in the… uh, hold on a second. Ann?
ANN	Yeah.
ALMANDA	You're supposed to be at the assembly.
ANN	Yeah, I know.
ALMANDA	What are you doing here?
ANN	It's boring.

ALMANDA	Doesn't matter. Go. Now. I've got work to do.
ANN	Miss…
ALMANDA	I'm serious, Ann, come on, out.
ANN	I think, uhm… I think, uhm… I think… I have a… there's somebody I know, and I think she needs help.
ALMANDA	What kind of help?
ANN	I can't say.
ALMANDA	Is it you?
ANN	No.
ALMANDA	Who is it?
ANN	Okay, like… the thing is… okay… like… this is really seriously… I mean, you can't let this person know that this came from me, a'ight?
ALMANDA	Is it Violet?
ANN	You didn't hear that from me.
ALMANDA	Is she pregnant?
ANN	No.
ALMANDA	What is it then?
ANN	So you're gonna do this then, a-ight?
ALMANDA	Do what?

ANN   Peace out, Miss M.

                       ANN leaves. Lights down on ALMANDA, up
                       on THOMAS who is on the phone.

THOMAS   Just got the call a couple of minutes ago. The
                       decision's coming any time now. Gotta get
                       things in motion, got emails to send. Can I
                       send them? No. Why? Email is down. I called
                       IT, told them it's an emergency, and...

                       Hold on a second. Hello, yes, this is Thomas
                       Matthews from the Crown attorney's office,
                       is Melina there? Sure.

                       Back to the audience.

                       I've been here at the University and Dundas
                       office for about three years now. I have no
                       idea who half these people are. There's about
                       a hundred lawyers here, and I have no idea
                       who that woman is over there. Oui, allô
                       Melina, c'est Thomas. Pas pire, pas pire. Je
                       vas avoir besoin le dossier Moseby. Oui, oui,
                       pas de problème.

                       He's on hold again.

                       I checked out the uh... the Toronto Police on
                       Wikipedia. And I have to admit, it's... well...
                       hold on, I'll pull it up.

                       He goes to his computer, pulls up a website.

                       Uh... this is a good section. Uh... "In 1859,
                       Toronto police stood by while enraged
                       Toronto firemen burned down a visiting
                       circus when its clowns jumped a lineup at a

local whorehouse. After this incident, the entire Toronto police force, along with its chief, were fired." Beautiful.

Back on phone.

Allô? Oui. Okay. Oui. Merci, Elizabeth. Melina! Melina. Désolé. À bientôt.

Hangs up.

Man I hate when I do that. Anyway... there was a link to corruption, that led me to the drug-squad officers that were charged. Constable Ned Maodus, trafficking cocaine. Staff Sergeant John Schertzer, extortion; Constable Steve Correia, extortion. You think that's bad, how about this, Rick McIntosh, head of the police association resigns, for what? He's charged with running a protection racket. And then I found this... Peter Shoniker, the GREAT Peter Shoniker, former Crown attorney, here in this office, was charged in 2002. Four counts of money laundering. And what stopped me cold was...

PETER enters.

PETER   Hey, Bogsy!

THOMAS   Was uh... he was a...

PETER   Karaoke at the Fox and Fiddle Thursday night. Don't make any plans.

To the audience.

THOMAS   Hold on a second.

PETER	Poutine!
THOMAS	Pete!
PETER	Charter motion in yet?
THOMAS	Not yet.
PETER	A successful charter motion counts as a loss.
THOMAS	Dude, how's Caledonia?
PETER	Peachy.
THOMAS	That Native treaty should be wrapped up sometime around the Leaf's Stanley Cup win.
PETER	Who're you up against?
THOMAS	Simon Phillips.
PETER	Ah. Clockwork.
THOMAS	You know him?
PETER	Oh yeah. Tell him Cashin wants to know if Rosa Luxemburg has given him a spit-roast yet.
THOMAS	I'll do that.
PETER	Seven all my friend.
THOMAS	Yeah yeah.
PETER	Seven all.

PETER leaves.

THOMAS	That's Peter Cashin. Of THE Cashins. Don't worry, I didn't know who they were either. They go all the way back to the Family Compact. UCC. U of T law school. For Peter, the Crown attorney's office is just one stop on the long road to becoming prime minister. And he's my main competition for that one spot on the murder unit. Some think the position is gonna go to him 'cause he's connected and white, and some think it's going to me cause I'm black and bilingual. It's a battle royale. And…

Phone rings.

Hold on a second. Hello. Yes, that's me. I have a charter motion coming through the pike today, yes. Has the motion come in? Could you check? Thanks.

To audience.

This could be it. Whew. Breath. What I love is having that competition. It forces you to…

To phone

Hello? What? Oh. Okay. Well, when it does come in, send me an email and… NO sorry, call. CALL me.

WILLIAM enters.

At this number. Correct. Yes. Kay. Thanks.

Hangs up. To WILLIAM.

Can I help you?

WILLIAM	IT.
THOMAS	Yes!
WILLIAM	You have the email problem?
THOMAS	YES. I do.
WILLIAM	Can I get in there?
THOMAS	Certainly.

THOMAS lets WILLIAM sit at his desk.

WILLIAM	Thanks.

THOMAS speaks to the audience, taking care not to be overheard by WILLIAM.

THOMAS	We have a brother in IT. Well look at that.
WILLIAM	So you're having problems with attachments?
THOMAS	No no. I can't send anything.
WILLIAM	Ah.
THOMAS	I get stuff, but I can't send.
WILLIAM	Could you write your password down on a piece of paper?
THOMAS	Okay.

THOMAS writes his password down. WILLIAM reads it and finds it funny.

WILLIAM	I'm gonna try something here.

To audience.

THOMAS — It's funny, I'm standing here and the thought strikes me, "Why don't I have more black friends." And then I look around and think. "Well, why don't I have any friends?" I have no friends. I have work acquaintances. I have people I speak to. I have no friends. For years it's just been me and my wife and busting our asses to put a down payment on a place, and...

WILLIAM — Ah, okay, this is gonna take about ten minutes.

THOMAS — You do whatchu gotta do, brotha.

THOMAS realizes how pathetic he truly is.

WILLIAM — Sure.

Phone rings. It's THOMAS's boss.

THOMAS — Hello? No. It's not in yet. No. I'll call you when it does. Yes.

Hangs up.

WILLIAM — Big case?

THOMAS — Yup.

WILLIAM — I'm just doing a reinstall of Outlook. You wanna keep the old password?

THOMAS — Yup.

WILLIAM — You got it.

THOMAS	I'm sorry, I didn't get your name.
WILLIAM	William. William Willis.
THOMAS	So all through school, you got the "Whatchu talkin 'bout, Willis."
WILLIAM	I still do.
THOMAS	And people think they're funny.
WILLIAM	They think they're REAL funny.

The phone rings. THOMAS *answers.* MARY *on the other side of the stage in silhouette.*

THOMAS	Yes.
MARY ANN	I'm sorry, is this Matthews... Thomas Matthews?
THOMAS	Yes, that's me.
MARY ANN	I'm sorry, I've been trying to get in touch with you and I'm a bit under the gun.
THOMAS	Okay.
MARY ANN	My name is Mary Shadd, I'm writing an article for the *Star* about youth, gun violence, and the law and I was hoping to talk to you about...
THOMAS	Right, yeah, I got your message. I'm kinda busy so...
MARY ANN	Could we meet tomorrow for lunch?

THOMAS	Can't do tomorrow.
MARY ANN	How about today?
THOMAS	I'm waiting for...
MARY ANN	I hear you lawyer types like to meet at Hy's.
THOMAS	Sure. Hy's. And uh... I might have to run.
MARY ANN	This shouldn't take long at all.
THOMAS	Okay, uhm sure. What's your name again?
MARY ANN	Mary. See you in forty minutes?
THOMAS	See you there.

Lights down on THOMAS *and up on* AL-MANDA, *who enters marking assignments.*

ALMANDA	...and so I head into the staff room for lunch, and there's a group of Chatty Cathies going on and on about the school closures and I felt it kick. For the second time, I felt it kick. Her. Or him. They say spicy food can... anyway. So then suddenly I've got these cosmic thoughts going through my head, like, "We are so fragile. Human beings are so..."
VIOLET	You wanted to see me?
ALMANDA	Violet?
VIOLET	You said you wanted to see me.
ALMANDA	Yes. That's right. Sit down, please.

VIOLET	I can't stay too long. I've got to be someplace.
ALMANDA	I'm looking for the poetry assignment. Violet?
VIOLET	What.
ALMANDA	I'm looking for the poetry assignment. Is it finished? Do you have it? Can I see it?
VIOLET	Hmm.
ALMANDA	It's ten percent of your mark.

VIOLET sucks her teeth.

Listen, I've said this to you before. You're very smart.

VIOLET	Yeah yeah yeah.
ALMANDA	You ARE. You just have to apply yourself.
VIOLET	Yeah yeah.
ALMANDA	It's true! But after a while, I'll get sick and tired of telling you and I'll stop and I won't care any more.
VIOLET	Well then stop.
ALMANDA	Everything okay at home?
VIOLET	What?
ALMANDA	At home. Everything okay?
VIOLET	What business is that of yours?!

ALMANDA	You just seem... like you don't... if there's something you need to talk to me about you can tell me.
VIOLET	Everything's fine at home.
ALMANDA	You sure?
VIOLET	Yes, I'm sure. Can I go now?!
ALMANDA	Okay. Well... okay. Fine. Go.
	VIOLET heads to the door.
	Wait. Hold on. I just changed my mind. For you and you alone, the poem is worth one hundred percent. You fail this, you fail the whole assignment. Your at thirty-seven percent for the year. You fail this, you don't get out of grade ten.
VIOLET	What?!
ALMANDA	That's the deal. Now get out.
VIOLET	You can't do that!
ALMANDA	You don't think I can do that?
VIOLET	That's unfair!
ALMANDA	You know what? I don't care. You're lazy, you're arrogant, you don't want to be here anyway, so take the failure, see you next year.
VIOLET	You don't mess with me, bitch!
ALMANDA	And you just got a detention.

VIOLET	Detention my ass, I'll shoot you in your face, bitch!
ALMANDA	Don't you DARE threaten me!
VIOLET	What, you want to call the cops?!
ALMANDA	I WANT YOU TO DO THE ASSIGNMENT! I want you to write... I don't care if it's a damn haiku. Write me a poem about your life! How you honestly feel. Right now. No one will see it but me. I will not judge you. You want to write a poem about how much you hate my guts? Do it! Because you're a brilliant young woman who could take over the world, but you can't if you don't get off your ass and do the work!
VIOLET	Whatevah.

VIOLET leaves.

ALMANDA	I've got to get the hell out of this city. I've got to.

Lights down on ALMANDA. Lights up on SOLOMON. He sits in a chair. SIMON bursts into the room, pulling out files.

SIMON	Hey. Solomon! You're here. Great. Sorry about... they closed the freaking Gardiner. There was ice on the... apparently there are big sheets of ice on the CN tower. Big chunks of ice falling on cars and... they closed the Gardiner. Sorry about that.

SOLOMON shrugs.

So. Long time no see. How's your sister?

> *SOLOMON nods.*

Good?

> *SOLOMON nods. SIMON pulls out a blank affidavit.*

Great. So, as I said, I met with the Crown attorney. And I just want to talk to you about a few things. It's been a while, so I thought it'd be a good idea to connect. Touch base. Nothing too big. Okay?

> *SOLOMON nods.*

Great. Now, I fully expect the charter motion to go through. When it does, I want to move as quickly as possible. Now, we're going to need affidavits from people you know.

> *SIMON hands SOLOMON the affidavit. SOLOMON takes it, looks at it, then hands it back to SIMON.*

A page, page and a half maybe, of statements by... oh, your sister, your... any old teachers... you go to church?

> *Shakes his head.*

Or even... if you're close with anyone who goes to... anyway. It's just something to start thinking about.

> *SIMON hands the affidavit back to SOLOMON.*

Now.

SOLOMON begrudgingly takes it.

And this... okay. If the motion doesn't go through then we go to trial. Chances are, the Crown attorney is going to send some cops to your door to ask questions. To intimidate you. If he does, call me. Don't freak out, don't say anything, just call me. Okay?

SOLOMON nods.

Listen, what that cop did to you that night was wrong. She had no right to stop you. No right to question you. You are a citizen of this country, a free citizen, and I'm going to do whatever it takes to make sure you get justice. Kay? Okay?

SOLOMON nods.

So... you uh... do you... do you have any questions?

SOLOMON   I need a job.

SIMON   Ah...

SOLOMON   You know where I can get a job?

SIMON   You know what? That's a good question. That's a good question. Let me... I'll have my... I have someone here that can help. Uh... she's not here, she's not going to be back for an hour, but I've got your cell number and I'll do what I can. How about that.

SOLOMON   I need to get paid.

SIMON	Yeah. I.... Yeah. I understand.
	Lights down on SIMON *and* SOLOMON. *Lights up on* THOMAS.
THOMAS	So I'm walking through Hy's and I remember why I hate coming here.
CHORUS 4	Thomas!
THOMAS	Hey. How's it going?
CHORUS 4	Coming to karaoke?
THOMAS	Uh, not sure. Maybe.
CHORUS 4	You're missing out.
THOMAS	Lawyers everywhere, half their names I don't remember.
CHORUS 1	Hey, Matthews.
THOMAS	Hey, how's the wife?
CHORUS 1	I wouldn't know. We divorced three weeks ago.
THOMAS	Oh right! You told me that. Yes. Sorry.
CHORUS 1	It's okay. It's fine.
THOMAS	I like to think of myself as a real people person, but I don't think I could prove that hypothesis with any valid evidence.
MARY ANN	Mr. Matthews

THOMAS	And I find myself walking towards this… beautiful, stunningly beautiful, black woman. And… my wedding ring…
MARY ANN	Mary Shadd.
THOMAS	I left it on the kitchen counter. I took it off to wash the…
MARY ANN	Is this okay?
THOMAS	I beg your pardon?
MARY ANN	Did you want to move? Or…
THOMAS	No, this is fine. This is fine.
MARY ANN	Thanks again for doing this. I know it's really short notice…
THOMAS	What's this about again?
MARY ANN	The *Star* is doing a series called "War on Poverty," and I'm doing an article on guns and youth and cops and race and all that fun stuff. You read the *Star*?
THOMAS	*Globe and Mail.* They tend to use words with more than two syllables.
MARY ANN	Ah. I see. Wow. Well…
THOMAS	You ever thought of writing for the *Globe*?
MARY ANN	Uh no. No, I haven't.
THOMAS	How did you get my name?

MARY ANN	Enzo at NOW *Magazine*. He did the piece on illegal immigrants working in construction.
THOMAS	Right, right. Yes. I remember.
	She pulls out a voice recorder.
MARY ANN	You don't mind if I record this, do you?
THOMAS	Yes, I do.
MARY ANN	Oh. Well. There's no reason to... I just record it so that I don't have to use a notepad.
THOMAS	No recording.
MARY ANN	Oookay.
	She pulls out a notepad.
THOMAS	And at any time, I might have to run.
MARY ANN	I understand. Been there, done that. Order anything you want, it's on me.
TIIOMAS	NO, no. I can take care of it.
MARY ANN	I know you can. But you won't, I will.
THOMAS	Well okay. Sure.
	Lights down on THOMAS and MARY ANN. Lights up on SIMON.
SIMON	And so I get out of the cab at Jarvis and what... Gerrard. I've done this before. A couple of times. On my lunch, I've gone to the

hotel on the corner. The dive. Used to be a really scuzzy dive, but they've fixed it up a bit, so now it's just a dive. And I've gone up to the front desk. A couple of times. And I've asked how much the room is. And I usually just walk away. But the kids are in daycare. Both of them. They're fine. They're well taken care of. My wife's in Buffalo with her family. And I think I'm doing this. I think I actually... I just... the motion's coming. I'll get the call. I have my cell. And if ever I'm going to do this, it's going to be once. And it's going to be right now.

CHORUS 5   Hi, can I help you?

SIMON   Yes, I uhm. Could I get a room?

CHORUS 5   Certainly.

SIMON   And they get me to sign something and I use a false name, and I head up to the room. Not bad. It'll do.

                He sits on the bed.

                This is exactly the kind of thing you can get busted for. She could be a cop. Or she could rob you. From what I hear, you can call, she comes over. Her boyfriend bursts in, says he's gonna kill you unless you hand over your wallet. Then they've got your wallet, they know where you live, they know where your kids live. Okay, you know what? I gotta go.

                He gets up.

I gotta... okay, well, I've.... If I'm standing here not doing anything, then I'm not doing anything wrong. I'll check my messages.

Pulls out cellphone, calls in for messages.

I know better too. I mean, what do I expect. She's gonna come in here. And she's gonna to be some... tortured drug addict. It's not like, as a kid, she dreamed of being a... oh. New message. This could be it... freaking telemarketers! Now they've got a machine to call and leave a message on my machine! Incredible.

Puts away phone.

Do I really want to do this? What time is it now? Okay, so... all right. All right.

He pulls out a newspaper clipping.

Lets see. I shouldn't use my cell. I should use the hotel phone.

He goes to the hotel phone, starts to dial.

I can't believe I'm doing this. I'm just about to do something horrible that I will regret for the... I'm... I uh... I uh...

Lights down on SIMON. Lights up on ALMANDA.

ALMANDA   I'm out of the cab, I tip him nothing because he took me across Queen Street when I told him five times not to and I guess we women don't know anything about traffic in the city and he just pissed me off. Breathe. Calm down. Let it go. And now I'm doing my best to half run to the elevator of the Women's College Hospital. And my bladder is full because that's what the ultrasound needs to see the baby, so I... excuse me! Hold the elevator please! Thank you! Thank you so much. Got my Dominique Michel, got a couple of essays to look over, and I've got Violet's poem. Not looking forward to it. Uh, this is my floor. I'm sure she lets me have it. I don't understand the sign, am I supposed to wait over here, or...

CHORUS 2 get's ALMANDA's name slightly wrong.

CHORUS 2   Almaaanda Matthews.

ALMANDA corrects her.

ALMANDA   Almanda. Yes. That's me.

CHORUS 2   Dr. Barret will be ready to see you in a moment. Over here please.

ALMANDA   Thank you. And uh... what was I saying...

CHORUS 2   Fill this out please.

She hands ALMANDA a clipboard.

ALMANDA   Sure.

ALMANDA sits.

Oh jeez. Oh my legs. Okay. I'll just... I'll just... I take out Violet's poem. I'll just take a peek. Get it over and done with. Then I'll be able to relax and look at the essays then get to my book.

She opens VIOLET's poem. VIOLET enters.

VIOLET   My life is like a roller coaster. Everything seems to go wrong.

ALMANDA   Uh...

VIOLET   He said he would shoot my family. If I did not say yes.

ALMANDA   Oh no.

VIOLET   Sometimes I feel like I'm not supposed to be around.

ALMANDA   Oh God.

VIOLET   I have no explanation for why he...

CHORUS 2   We're ready for you now.

ALMANDA   I'm sorry?

CHORUS 2   We're ready for you now.

ALMANDA   Uh, okay. Sure. Sure.

Lights down on ALMANDA, VIOLET, and CHORUS 2. Lights up on THOMAS and MARY.

THOMAS   How the hell did your parents end up in Brantford!?

MARY ANN   My mom is like, Canadian Canadian all the way back to the underground railroad...

THOMAS	Get out!
MARY ANN	And my dad's Guyanese.
THOMAS	My stepdad's Guyanese!
MARY ANN	So you know about the *Koi Koi*?
THOMAS	What the hell is that?
MARY ANN	Before you get married, you and your partner sit down and all the elders sit around you in a circle and they sing sexually explicit songs to you.
THOMAS	Eeeeh.
MARY ANN	So your stepdad is Guyanese, your parents are...
THOMAS	Jamaican.
MARY ANN	They must be very proud.
THOMAS	Yeah.
MARY ANN	Now how many other people of colour are there in the office?
THOMAS	In the whole office?
MARY ANN	Yeah.
THOMAS	I... couldn't tell you.
MARY ANN	You don't know?

THOMAS	A few. We've got about a hundred attorneys, and I've never... call the office. Someone there can answer that for you.
MARY ANN	Any problems growing up?
THOMAS	How do you mean?
MARY ANN	Racial incidents.
THOMAS	Not really.
MARY ANN	None?
THOMAS	Well, nothing important.
MARY ANN	When I was in high school I entered the beauty pageant as a joke. I came in second. Then one of the judges told me I actually came in first but someone "Didn't feel that a nigger girl is the proper representation..."
THOMAS	Oh no.
MARY ANN	"...of the beauty of Brantford."
THOMAS	What'd you do?
MARY ANN	They told me to enter again and I would win for sure...
THOMAS	And you...
MARY ANN	I entered again. And I lost. Again.
THOMAS	Ouch!

MARY ANN	Yeah.
THOMAS	Well, you... you've done... just fine for yourself.
MARY ANN	Thanks. Any other black kids in high school?
THOMAS	What does this have to do with...
MARY ANN	Just background stuff. I probably won't use any of it.
THOMAS	There were a few. There was this girl. Lorrie. I had a crazy-assed crush on her. But she was in grade twelve, I was in grade nine, it... wasn't meant to be.
MARY ANN	I'm sure you've done just fine since then.
THOMAS	Oh I'm married and about to have a kid.
MARY ANN	What's your wife's background?
THOMAS	French. Franco-Ontarian.

MARY ANN writing furiously.

MARY ANN	When's the baby due?
THOMAS	In a while. She's at the end of her first trimester. You're not going to... make a thing about that are you?
MARY ANN	About what?
THOMAS	Nothing.
MARY ANN	No, tell me, about what?

THOMAS	Oh just... nothing. Forget it.
MARY ANN	So how does a left-leaning black lawyer from Ottawa end up defending a white police officer against charges of racial profiling?
THOMAS	Well, first off the defendant wasn't racially profiled. Second...
MARY ANN	Oh come off it!
THOMAS	...the officer was performing her duty.
MARY ANN	You don't actually believe that do you?
THOMAS	If you have evidence that contradicts the officer's statement...
MARY ANN	I've got the ACC's report on profiling that shows a systemic pattern of...
THOMAS	That report can say whatever it wants. My client didn't profile anyone.
MARY ANN	Have you ever been profiled?
THOMAS	I'd rather not talk about it.
MARY ANN	Ah! So that's your deal.
THOMAS	What's my deal?
MARY ANN	All your white friends in high school said they like you because you're not one of those angry black guys, and they ask you if you tan during the summer and you smile and tell them you sincerely like the guitar riff to "Sweet Home Alabama" even though

they diss Neil Young, and you don't like rap and hip hop because it's too violent, and you found yourself a nice Canadian wife who will give you children with good hair, and you will come into work with people you barely know, and you don't want to know them because you're scared, and you should be scared, because if you said out loud what you truly feel, what you really, honestly feel inside, then you would never get the promotion and the car and the house and the cottage and all the other trappings of the middle-class Canadian dream that you feel so entitled to.

THOMAS   Our parents came to this country when it was a hundred times more racist than it is today. And they became doctors, engineers; my dad worked at the Department of Defence, and my mother ran the emergency room at the Civic. And these kids out there, these thugs, they are pissing all over that legacy.

MARY ANN   Interesting.

THOMAS   Our parents worked their asses off to provide for us, to open doors for us, and these kids, they kill each other. For what? Why? Guns are completely and totally unacceptable. Period.

MARY ANN   Why do you think you were put on this case?

THOMAS   Because I bust my ass to be the best there is.

MARY ANN   Wouldn't it be nice to live in a world where you didn't have to work twice as hard so that you could be seen as being equal.

THOMAS	I don't want to be seen as being equal. I want to be seen as being superior. And you only get that by working your ass off.
	THOMAS's phone rings.
MARY ANN	You gotta run?
THOMAS	Yeah, I've got to run. Thanks for lunch. Let me know what happens with the article.
MARY ANN	I'm going to email you the ACC's report on racial profiling.
THOMAS	Sure. Do that.
	Lights down on MARY ANN and THOMAS. Lights up on SIMON walking the street.
SIMON	Taxi. Taxi! What was I thinking? Taxi! I paid eighty bucks for a room I didn't even use. That's diaper money, that's food, babysitter, that's... aw man! What's my... problem. Taxi!
	GURDIT the taxi driver enters.
GURDIT	Where are you going?
SIMON	I'm uh... Filmores.
GURDIT	Okay.
	SIMON gets in the taxi.
SIMON	Grab a beer. Chill out. What have I done? She's gonna get to the door, she's gonna knock. No one's gonna be there. She'll be pissed, but so

what. It's the right thing to do. I mean, I can't really… I'm married. I'm not that guy. That guy who…

To the taxi driver.

Could you uh, sorry, excuse me?

GURDIT   Yes?

SIMON   Could you turn on the radio please?

GURDIT   Sure.

CFRB HOST 1   Are you kidding me? If ever there was a time this country needs to give consumers a tax break…

CFRB HOST 2   If someone would just get in there and start running this government like a business…

SIMON   Like a business?

CFRB HOST 2   Get rid of the inefficiencies, cut the fat…

SIMON   Like a business? Like what… Enron? Nortel? You want to run the government like flipping Nortel?

GURDIT   Six seventy-five.

SIMON   Here. Keep it.

SIMON gets out of the taxi.

GURDIT   Have a good day.

SIMON	How efficient was the flipping IMF in Argentina in 2001?
	SIMON enters strip club. Bartender JEFFREY Reodica takes his jacket.
JEFFREY	Hey, brothah Simon…
SIMON	Jeffrey…
JEFFREY	Double rum and coke?
SIMON	Pint of Stella.
JEFFREY	You got it, Pontiac.
	JENNIFER walks up to SIMON. Rush's "Tom Sawyer" kicks in.
SIMON	How freaking efficient was the IMF in Kenya in the nineties. But no!!! All hail Milton Friedman. All hail privatization, deregulation…
JENNIFER	Hey, lover boy.
SIMON	Jennifer.
JENNIFER	I've just gotta finish this and I'll be right with ya.
SIMON	Trickle Down Theory, Common Sense Revolution…
JENNIFER	If you could just move your leg, sweetheart, I can…

SIMON moves his legs. She moves in between his legs and starts to dance.

SIMON The miracle in Chile... then Pinochet, then Reagan... oh gosh, Jennifer, you're a... then Thatcher, then Mulroney, then... oh honey, then... oh my lord. I uh... uh... oh good lord, look at you... look at you...

SIMON's cellphone rings.

I've uh... I'm sorry, I've got to take this.

JENNIFER It's okay.

JENNIFER keeps dancing.

SIMON Thérèse. Hey, I'll be back in the office in about forty. Yeah. What? I can barely hear you, what? It's in? Talk to me. What's it say? Kay. Okay. Kay. What did... kay. I'll be right there.

He hangs up. His heart is broken yet again. This time worse than ever before.

JENNIFER You all right, darlin'?

SIMON Jennifer, dark freaking clouds of oppression rule this world.

Lights up on THOMAS, who is busy preparing his opening statement on a notepad.

THOMAS As I expected, the charter motion was rejected.

SIMON Dark, hard, silent, invisible fingers of oppression are reaching out right now, out into the universe.

Lights down on SIMON *and* JENNIFER. ROSE *enters.*

ROSE What is dis?!

THOMAS I sent two officers to ask Solomon some questions.

ROSE Ynaw ave nutn useful fi do!?

THOMAS And I struggle to supress a new, strange, simmering...

ROSE Comin round here disterbin my peace.

THOMAS I don't think I've ever felt like this before.

ROSE Ya disterbin my peace, ya hear me!?

THOMAS I have a ton of stuff to take care of, but...

ROSE Rawted.

Lights slowly down on ROSE.

THOMAS I don't... I don't have time to waste justifying myself to...

Lights up on ALMANDA.

ALMANDA Get on the streetcar at College and University and will NOBODY GIVE ME A DAMN SEAT?! Please. My feet are... never mind. It's fine. I've got the pictures of the ultrasound still in my hand, but I'm thinking about Violet's poem and what she described, and I'm lost. I mean, if it's true... I mean, do I have to do something?

Lights up on THOMAS, *at home in the kitchen running around.*

THOMAS   How can a loaf of bread go bad so quickly? What am I going to do? I can throw a President's Choice Vegetable Lasagna in the oven, but that's gonna take an hour, and she's going to want to eat the moment she gets in the door, and...

ALMANDA enters.

ALMANDA   Hey honey.

THOMAS   I'm so sorry, I was going to pick up a roasted chicken at Sobeys, I forgot.

ALMANDA   There's a President's Choice Lasagna in the freezer.

THOMAS   Yeah, and it'll take an hour.

He kisses her on the lips.

ALMANDA   Microwave it.

THOMAS   I thought you...

ALMANDA   I know, just do it. I'll be fine. Are there any carrots?

THOMAS   How was your day?

ALMANDA   Awful. Here's the ultrasound.

THOMAS   Wow.

ALMANDA   I think the head's there somewhere.

THOMAS	It looks beautiful.
	He kisses her.
ALMANDA	Yeah yeah. Did the charter thing happen?
THOMAS	Uh, yeah. It was rejected.
ALMANDA	And that's good for you, right?
THOMAS	Yeah it is. Before I forget, you should call your mom, she left a message on the machine if you want to hear it.
ALMANDA	Did you remember to get the licence sticker?
	He didn't.
THOMAS	Ah...
ALMANDA	Sacrament!
THOMAS	Monday. First thing Monday.
ALMANDA	You've been saying that for two weeks!
THOMAS	I know.
ALMANDA	It's like you don't listen to me!
THOMAS	I listen to you, I've been preoccupied.
ALMANDA	You think I haven't been preoccupied?! You think I haven't... I've got a kid who was forced at gunpoint to give some gangbanger a blow job and you think that doesn't preoccupy me?!
THOMAS	I've told you that you can use my car.

ALMANDA	I DON'T DRIVE STANDARD!
THOMAS	Honey, calm down…
ALMANDA	I don't want you to teach me to drive standard, I don't want to take a taxi, I want you to do what you say your going to do!
THOMAS	Well, you know what? Sometimes in life you don't get what you want!
ALMANDA	Is that so!
THOMAS	Trust me, I would have been ten times happier in my life if I was having a dark-skinned child with a dark-skinned wife and you would have been happier marrying some blue-eyed son of a bitch that could give you all the blond babies that you know you want deep down inside! Well, guess what! That ain't happening! You're married to me, and I'm married to you! That's the way it is! Deal with it!
ALMANDA	Uh…
	ALMANDA leaves. THOMAS realizes he's crossed the line.
THOMAS	You can't… hey! We're not done here. Hey! Honey! Come back! This is a… honey, come back, I…
	Hip-hop music. Lights down on THOMAS. Lights up on SOLOMON. He's got a microphone.
SOLOMON	All right, all right. Check it. One two one two. Fa REAL. This is me, Solomon Moseby,

a.k.a. Busy B, a.k.a. the Minute Man, a.k.a. Moon Nite, a.k.a. the Mighty Torrent of Hate and Truth and Love that'll all come raining down on all of y'all. Shout out Parkdale in the house! Cataraqui in tha house, Teesdale in tha house! MnL, Jane Finch, Black Creek, Scarlettville, Chester Le, *(His tone turns dark, threatening.)* Chalkfarm.

> *He makes a gun with his hand, points it at the imaginary Chalkfarm in the audience. Pulls the trigger. Smiles.*

This here's the Ballad of Busy B. Check it. One two one two. All right, all right. I'm gonna break this down for y'all. So y'all can bear witness. To see this.

Lord only knows you never wanna be this.
I got no voice and yet I must scream this.
I've got a soul, but y'all just look through me.
You wanna see the future but you're livin in
    the past.
You want the double feature but the flavour
    don't last
In a government apartment with a leak in
    every floor
You dream of something bigger, always
    wantin somethin more
And in my quiet moments when I am all alone.
I dream about the one day that will call me on
    the phone.
I see
All the different kinds of potentialities
And any one in a million of them could one
    day be me.
And so why you got to get all up and chill in
    my grill.

I see you with your gat and you thinkin you
  all that.
I see you in the club. I see you in the street.
Who told you, you could look at me like that?
Who told you, you could come into my
  universe and look at me like that. I raise em
  high, you gotta die.
I'll lay you low with a booyakah booyakah!
All the hos in the front.
I see your Niggahs in the corner.
I got my Niggahs on tha flo.
Simple as one, two, three, easy as ABC.

Gunfire.

CHORUS 2/4/5   He's running.

CHORUS 3   Christopher Holder, thirty-two, shot and
                 killed.

CHORUS 6   Aleem Rehmtulla, twenty-six, shot and
                 killed.

SOLOMON   I'm chasing you down to the front door.

CHORUS 2/4/5   Running.

SOLOMON   One of ya Niggahs lets fly with a barrage of
                 molten death.

CHORUS 6   Amon Beckles,

CHORUS 3   Jeffrey Black,

CHORUS 6   Michael Lewis, shot and killed.

CHORUS 2   We bear witness.

CHORUS 3	Paul Watson, thirty-three, shot and killed.
SOLOMON	I am out into the night, I am the Prince of Darkness. You got your Niggahs, I got my Niggahs, all tussling in the deep, dark blue black of the night, pullin at each other's hair, slappin at each othahs faces, blowing each others brains out!

SOLOMON finds his target.

CHORUS 6	Leroy Whittaker, forty-six, innocent bystander, shot and killed.
CHORUS 4	We bear witness.
CHORUS 3	Jamal Hemmings, seventeen.
CHORUS 5	We bear witness.
CHORUS 6	Nageeb Craig Henry, twenty-two.
CHORUS 2	We bear witness.
CHORUS 6	Tito Benjamin, twenty-nine.
CHORUS 4	We bear witness.
SOLOMON	And I've got you in my sights, I got to pop you off into oblivion and…
CHORUS 3/6	Bang.
SOLOMON	I'm hit.

CHORUS 4 turns on a laser pointer and points it at SOLOMON's body

CHORUS 4	Entry point: right costoclavicular ligament. Deflecting seventy-two degrees, exiting through right platysma muscle.
CHORUS 3/6	Bang.
	CHORUS 2/5 turn on laser pointers and point them at SOLOMON's body.
CHORUS 6	Bang.
	CHORUS 4 turns on a laser pointer and points it at SOLOMON's body.
CHORUS 4	Entry point: femoris muscle, deflected off the left femur.
SOLOMON	Oh shit.
CHORUS 3	Bang.
CHORUS 5	Entry point.
	CHORUS 4/5 turn on laser pointers and point them at SOLOMON's body.
CHORUS 2	Jawbone.
CHORUS 2	Vaporizing the retromandibular vein.
CHORUS 6	Solomon Moseby.
	CHORUS 6 brings a large board up behind SOLOMON with an outline of his body.
CHORUS 3	A.k.a. Busy B.
CHORUS 5	A.k.a....

CHORUS 2	The Mighty Torrent of Hate and Truth and Love...
CHORUS 5	Laying in a pool of his own blood.
SOLOMON	I got no voice, and yet I must scream. Peace.

> *SOLOMON and the CHORUS leave. The board with the outline remains with the lasers painting the body. Lights down.*

> *End of Act One.*

ACT TWO

Hospital. ROSE sitting, asleep. SIMON rushes in. He gently wakes her up.

SIMON   I'm sorry I'm late, I had to get someone to look after the kids.

ROSE   That's... uh...

SIMON   How's he doing?

ROSE   I... I don't know. Dem tell me to leave, but me kyan get in there. I...

SIMON   Stay right there.

ROSE   I just...

CHORUS 4 enters.

SIMON   Excuse me. Excuse me! I need to find out information on a Solomon Moseby.

CHORUS 4 He's in ICU. Someone will come out, wait right there.

CHORUS 4 leaves.

SIMON	But could you... stop for a second! Excuse me!
ROSE	It's all right, Mr. Phillips, dey say a doctor will be here, it's all right.
SIMON	You want anything?
ROSE	No, it's okay.
SIMON	Seriously, I can get you anything you want, you hungry?
ROSE	Uh... no.
SIMON	He's gonna be okay. This is a good hospital. They uh... it's gonna be okay.
ROSE	I try so hard, I do, I try so hard to look after him, take care of him but... and now I think, is this my fault?
SIMON	No it's not.
ROSE	I just don't know why he... I... why the hell someone would want to do that to my brod-dah. I mean, why? For what?
SIMON	And I find myself trying to go past all the platitudes, all the clichés that people say in situations like this. I say a few things here and there. Let the silences fall naturally. I tell her how...

CHORUS 4 walks up to ROSE.

CHORUS 4	Excuse me, Rose Moseby?

ROSE	Yeah.
CHORUS 4	We're gonna need you to fill this out.
ROSE	Okay.

CHORUS 4 leaves.

SIMON	I tell her how I used to put my poor mother through the ringer. I built this ramp once, and we used to ride our bikes up off this ramp, just for kicks, and one day.... Uh... so one day, I decided to hike the ramp up so high that uh... my brother... I thought it would be funny to watch him go high up in the air. Anyway, he hits the ramp, full speed, lands on the concrete, the back of his head splits open, blood everywhere, and uh... and uh, my mother... she's like a... an archetypical Austrian matriarchal powerhouse, and we're in the hospital, she's laying into me, and sitting there blaming herself, and uh... what can I say, boys just... we just take things to the edge, that's what we do.

CHORUS 5 enters.

CHORUS 5	Rose Fortune Moseby.
ROSE	Yes.
CHORUS 5	Come this way, please. Quickly.
ROSE	Uh, uh, yeah okay.

CHORUS 5 and ROSE leave. THOMAS enters.

SIMON	But platitudes are... empty. And...

THOMAS	Hey.
SIMON	Hey.
THOMAS	Got your message.
SIMON	Yeah, thanks for, uh…
THOMAS	Tell me the sister's name again?
SIMON	Rose.
THOMAS	How's Rose doing?
SIMON	As well as to be expected. How's your wife?
THOMAS	Good. Good. How're your girls?
SIMON	Well the youngest isn't hitting any of the major developmental milestones, but hey, her dad was a slow learner, so…
THOMAS	Let's talk, shall we?
SIMON	Yeah. Sure.
THOMAS	We are ready to drop all the charges, free and clear…
SIMON	On condition of…
THOMAS	He's got to name the shooter.
SIMON	Right. Of course.
THOMAS	We have reason to believe that Mr. Moseby knows his assailant, and we have reason to believe Mr. Moseby's assailant is a person of

great interest to another investigation.

SIMON   Ah. I see.

THOMAS   He names the shooter, he's free.

SIMON   Good for you. Well, I want a trial.

THOMAS   I beg your pardon?

SIMON   I want a trial.

THOMAS   You can't be serious.

SIMON   Dead serious. We are turning down the offer, in favour of a trial.

THOMAS   Your client... okay, you want to put your client in front of a jury.

SIMON   Damn right I do.

THOMAS   He's caught with a firearm.

SIMON   Yup.

THOMAS   He's in hospital because of a shootout in a club and you think a jury is going to give him money.

SIMON   They will when Officer MacGill testifies that she racially profiled my client.

THOMAS   And why would she do that?

SIMON   Because that's the only way you're gonna get the name of the man that shot my client.

THOMAS   Oh you son of a bitch.

SIMON	The sooner you give us the testimony, the sooner you get your guy.
THOMAS	But if she didn't profile him, she can't lie about it.
SIMON	If she didn't profile him, we wouldn't be here.
THOMAS	You've got to be out of your mind.
SIMON	That's the deal. My client talks if she talks.
THOMAS	Why don't you appeal the charter motion!
SIMON	The charter is a freaking joke. I want a trial.
THOMAS	I am not going to counsel the witness to lie.
SIMON	Then tell the witness I want her in my office first thing in the morning for cross examination.
THOMAS	You gonna be there or should I tell her to wait?
SIMON	You're a funny guy. Joke machine. Keep it up.
THOMAS	Your wish is my command, buddy. Your wish is my command.

THOMAS leaves, incredulous. SIMON is tired. Lights down. Lights up on ALMANDA.

ALMANDA	Taxi! Tax… I couldn't mark any of these poems last night. I was too… anyway. Sometimes I think about what it would be like to have a French partner in my life, what that would mean for our child, but… and he's going to

say he didn't mean it, and he's sorry, but...
I've got to stop thinking about it. Okay, think
of something else... think of... uh... let's see if
I can mark some of these while I'm...

> OFFICER MacGILL *knocks on the door.*
> *Lights down on* ALMANDA. *Lights up on*
> SIMON *in his office, he's working on some-*
> *thing, laying in wait, setting his trap.*

SIMON Come on in.

OFFICER MacGILL Simon Phillips?

SIMON Can I help you?

OFFICER MacGILL I'm Officer MacGill.

SIMON From...

OFFICER MacGILL The... Toronto Police.

SIMON Oh, yes. Right. Yes, yes. Come on in. Grab a
seat there, I've just... I've got a couple of these
happening this morning. You want a coffee or
something?

OFFICER MacGILL No thank you.

SIMON Sure?

OFFICER MacGILL Yes.

SIMON We've got a deal with the Tim Hortons across
the street. I make a call, a guy comes up here
in, like, two seconds.

OFFICER MacGILL No thank you.

SIMON	Are you sure?
OFFICER MacGILL	Yes.

SIMON picks up the phone.

SIMON	It's not a big deal, really.
OFFICER MacGILL	I'm sure.
SIMON	Fine. You sure? I could use some Timbits, a twenty pack, double-double. No? Fine.

SIMON puts the phone down.

Now, okay. Let's see what Mr. Einstein's gotten himself up to this time.

Opens file, reads it.

Huhuuuh doduhdoduhdododo. Oh, right. Now you claim to have entered the Golden Hands establishment and you saw my client in a reverse massage...

OFFICER MacGILL	Uh...
SIMON	And I'll be honest with ya, I have no idea how you could identify the bastard, I mean, look at this guy.
OFFICER MacGILL	I don't know what you're talking about.
SIMON	Are you kidding me? Look at this. He's like, midnight black. He's like blue black. Jesus. I don't know how the hell you could make out who the heck this guy is...

OFFICER MacGILL	I think you're confusing this case with something else.
SIMON	What?
OFFICER MacGILL	Solomon Moseby. Gun charges.
SIMON	Really? Who's this guy? Tariq Jamma jamma something or other...
OFFICER MacGILL	Could we get this process started? I've got...
SIMON	Oh sure, sure. Of course.
OFFICER MacGILL	It's a busy day for me, so...
SIMON	Okay, who's this guy. Solomon... what... Moseby. You guys already have a long file on him already or what?
OFFICER MacGILL	Uh no. We don't.
SIMON	You don't?
OFFICER MacGILL	No.
SIMON	Surprise surprise. Will wonders never cease. Okay, well, you know the drill; I'm going to ask you some questions, and you just answer them. I'm sure the Crown has told you not to lose your temper.
OFFICER MacGILL	Yes, he has.
SIMON	Yeah, well, I'll tell you right now, I'm not like other defence attorneys. I have a huge, HUGE respect for what you men and women have to go through, day in, day out.

OFFICER MacGILL	Gee, thanks.
SIMON	You put your life on the line every day. That's huge. Okay? Huge. So, what's your take? Drug dealer, crack addict, pimp, what do you think the deal is with this guy?
OFFICER MacGILL	I think... you are not as clever as you believe yourself to be.
SIMON	Kay.
OFFICER MacGILL	I'm sure in your job, you get to see the ass end of the police force. Day in, day out. I'm sure there was a time when you could snag a few bad apples with your little fun bag of tactics. But I'll tell you something, the vast majority of cops, vast majority, out there, are hard-working, stand-up, honest people. The days when the force was just a bunch of white guys is over. It's done. Every day I go into work, there's a guy from the Philippines, and one guy, his parents are from Iran, our dispatch-er's from China. These are people I depend on to save my life. And when I go out onto the street, I'm interacting with every walk of life, from every culture, from every part of the planet. You can think whatever you want about me, or the cops you've dealt with in the past, but I'll tell you, most police officers are good people. We are just trying, really hard, to do our job and to do it well.
	SIMON thinks. He takes the file he has on OFFICER MacGILL and places it calmly in front of her.
SIMON	Says here you studied at Dalhousie.

OFFICER MacGILL	Yup.
SIMON	What'd you take?

> OFFICER MacGILL *takes a quick look at the file then shoves it away.*

OFFICER MacGILL	Poli-sci.
SIMON	Moved to Toronto...
OFFICER MacGILL	Nineteen ninety-seven.
SIMON	Worked in a restaurant.
OFFICER MacGILL	Pauper's Pub, on Bloor near Bathurst.
SIMON	Waitress?
OFFICER MacGILL	Sous chef.
SIMON	Why'd you become a police officer?
OFFICER MacGILL	Got sick and tired of the hours, the heat, the chef. Figured if I could put in seven years there, I could do anything.
SIMON	Make any friends on the force?
OFFICER MacGILL	What?
SIMON	Friends. You have any friends at work?
OFFICER MacGILL	Uh, yeah. Sure.
SIMON	Who?
OFFICER MacGILL	What do you mean?

SIMON	Name them. Name your friends.
OFFICER MacGILL	Oh. Uh, Clara.
SIMON	What's her full name?
OFFICER MacGILL	Clara Brett Martin.

SIMON takes the file and writes in it.

SIMON	Is she a close friend?
OFFICER MacGILL	Uh... close. Sure.
SIMON	How close?
OFFICER MacGILL	Uh, I don't know... close.
SIMON	Have a boyfriend?
OFFICER MacGILL	I don't think that's relevant.
SIMON	You and Clara very close?
OFFICER MacGILL	Are you calling me a dyke?
SIMON	I'm simply asking you a question, you and Clara, are you close?
OFFICER MacGILL	Just because I don't have a boyfriend and I've got a close female buddy, that doesn't mean that I'm a dyke.
SIMON	I'm not saying you are, but it would be tough if you were, wouldn't it.
OFFICER MacGILL	I'm not, so I wouldn't know.

SIMON	I'm guessing the atmosphere there is pretty intensely homophobic. Am I right? You've got a lot of testosterone all over the place. As a straight woman, you'd have to butch it up, just to prove you're one of the guys, is that right?
OFFICER MacGILL	Ah no.
SIMON	They don't want you to be a woman, they want you to be a man. Act like a man, police like a man.
OFFICER MacGILL	That doesn't make sense.
SIMON	What doesn't make…
OFFICER MacGILL	There is no way to police like a man or a woman.
SIMON	Own any rap music?
OFFICER MacGILL	What?
SIMON	Rap music. Do you have any in your CD collection?
OFFICER MacGILL	Oh you've got to be joking.
SIMON	Answer the question.
OFFICER MacGILL	Yes, that's right. My intense hatred of the misogyny in rap music sent me over the edge and now I've got to cuff every black guy I see.
SIMON	Listen here, honey, in this scenario, all you do is answer my questions. I talk, you answer. Got it, toots? No sarcasm, no smart remarks. Save those for your little friend.

OFFICER MacGILL   No. You listen here, you little prick. I know
                    what the deal is. You want me to say that I lied
                    about seeing him drive erratically, well guess
                    what, I didn't lie! I didn't. I didn't racially
                    profile anyone! I never would! But you know
                    what?! Even if I had profiled the guy, even if I
                    had, at least he didn't get shot that night! At
                    least he didn't get shot, he didn't shoot some-
                    body, he didn't shoot randomly into a build-
                    ing, into the street, killing innocent people.
                    That night, the night he spent behind bars,
                    was probably the safest he's been in MONTHS.
                    And I don't expect a fucking thank you, but
                    your fucking welcome.

                    SIMON starts to write furiously.

SIMON   Okay, that's excellent. Thanks, you can go.

OFFICER MacGILL   What are you writing?

SIMON   Officer MacGill, great meeting you.

OFFICER MacGILL   But…

SIMON   I'm done. You can go.

OFFICER MacGILL   Fine. You know what? That's just fine. Do
                    your worst.

                    Lights down on SIMON *and* OFFICER Mac-
                    GILL. *Lights up on* THOMAS.

THOMAS   And so I'm taking the elevator down to the
                    main floor to get the worst coffee in Toronto,
                    from the doughnut shop by the front lobby,
                    and why the hell did I read that article? Why
                    did I read it?

MARY ANN	Holding his head forward, with a look of entitlement that stems from his upper-middle-class childhood in the burbs of Ottawa...
THOMAS	I didn't have to read it. I knew I shouldn't have read it.
MARY ANN	By "part of the problem," I mean that he is one of the chosen. One of the few who have "made it."
THOMAS	It's that snide... tone of...
MARY ANN	Who doesn't understand this generation of lost youth and why they haven't just pulled themselves together and achieve like he did. Like his parents did.
THOMAS	Some of it is a lie.
MARY ANN	Even though he admits that there are no other people of colour in the Crown attorney's office.
THOMAS	I didn't say that. What I said was...
MARY ANN	Most black youth don't even think that it's possible to dream about anything but guns, drugs, and being a hip-hop superstar...
THOMAS	And some of it...
MARY ANN	Perhaps if he tried to see the world through Solomon's eyes, just once, instead of trying to teach him a lesson...
THOMAS	Some of it...

	PETER Cashin enters. Lights down on MARY.
PETER	Hey! Poutine!
THOMAS	Oh for...
PETER	Listen. I saw the article. Don't sweat it.
THOMAS	I won't.
PETER	Last year I had Jeffrey Simpson at the *Globe* call me an "unconscionable, grasping reprobate, whose vapidity is equalled only by his ambition."
THOMAS	Not bad.
PETER	Everybody's behind you. Wear it like a badge of honour.
THOMAS	Hey, how's Caledonia?
PETER	All good things must come to an end, my friend.
THOMAS	You're gonna have those treaties signed by, what, lunch?
	PETER leaves.
PETER	All good things must come to an end.
THOMAS	Uh. I should uh... I have to uh...
	Lights down on THOMAS. Lights up on MACGILL.

OFFICER MacGILL	I head down the hall. Which number is it again? I keep forgetting. I'm so behind in all my reports. I get to my desk in the morning and I can hear the sergeant reading out the parade for the day. And all I want to do is to get back out on the street.

She's now lost. She pulls out a piece of paper with the room number on it.

Am I supposed to... ah. Here we go.

She enters the room.

He's not here. Yeah. This is it. Hmmm. Anyway. All I want to do is get to the end of my shift and get to a bar and down a nice Cab Sav. Half litre. And I can't. I've got another damned sensitivity training course at the police college. And I do it, I show up and I don't complain, no matter how patronizing, no matter how

THOMAS enters.

THOMAS	Elsie.
OFFICER MacGILL	Yes?
THOMAS	Sorry about being late.
OFFICER MacGILL	It's fine.
THOMAS	I had to... there've been a few developments in the case and I had to talk to a couple of people.

OFFICER MacGILL	That doesn't sound... good.
THOMAS	Yeah, well, it isn't.
OFFICER MacGILL	Okay.
THOMAS	You talked to Simon.
OFFICER MacGILL	Yes, I did.
THOMAS	What did I tell you about losing your temper?
OFFICER MacGILL	Yeah, I kinda got a little heated at the end there.
THOMAS	Yes, you did.
OFFICER MacGILL	Is it a problem?
THOMAS	It's not your biggest problem.
OFFICER MacGILL	What's my biggest problem?
THOMAS	I don't believe your testimony.
OFFICER MacGILL	Oh.
THOMAS	I actually never did. Inside. For a number of reasons. Some of them have nothing to do with you, and obviously that's not fair. But my job has nothing to do with you. My job is to represent the Crown and her interests.
OFFICER MacGILL	Listen, I see where this is... oh, God... I see where this is going, and I uh...
THOMAS	Now of course, I'm not supposed to tell you any of this. I'm supposed to use your

	testimony to win the case. However, I am now in a position where that... has become... very hard for me to do.
OFFICER MacGILL	What does that mean?
THOMAS	The guy that shot Solomon, he's someone the RCMP have been after for a long, long time.
OFFICER MacGILL	Ah. Right. Okay.
THOMAS	Now, if Solomon would tell the RCMP that this guy tried to kill him...
OFFICER MacGILL	They'd be happy.
THOMAS	You should understand that if you act willingly, it will be... better for you in the long run.
OFFICER MacGILL	Oh Jesus. I mean. Come on. I can't lose my job. Mr. Matthews, I really can't. My dad... there's nobody else who... he needs someone to take care of him and... if I... and I love this job. I love it. And uh... I love what I do. I can't lose this job. I mean, what are you asking me to do... I mean...
THOMAS	You say the defendant was driving erratically.
OFFICER MacGILL	Mr. Matthews, I...
THOMAS	Was he drunk?
OFFICER MacGILL	No.
THOMAS	How did you find that out?
OFFICER MacGILL	After... I was able to asses that he wasn't drunk.

THOMAS	How? Did you give him a Breathalyzer?
OFFICER MacGILL	No.
THOMAS	In your testimony, you said you thought he might be drunk and you don't give him a Breathalyzer?
OFFICER MacGILL	By the time I had discovered the weapon...
THOMAS	That was after you pulled him out of the car.
OFFICER MacGILL	Sorry?

He looks for his notes.

THOMAS	You asked him for his licence and registration. You pulled him out of the car. Then you find the gun. That's your testimony.
OFFICER MacGILL	If that's what you have written down there, then sure.
THOMAS	Are there certain procedures you can follow to determine if a driver is drunk?
OFFICER MacGILL	Yes.
THOMAS	Did you do any of them?
OFFICER MacGILL	No.
THOMAS	Why not?
OFFICER MacGILL	He wasn't behaving drunk. He was behaving odd.

THOMAS	So then you lied, you didn't think he was drunk.
OFFICER MacGILL	No! He just—I thought at first he was drunk, but as I was walking up to the car, he was pulling at something under the dashboard. It turned out to be the change tray. I thought it was a gun.
THOMAS	That wasn't in your testimony.
OFFICER MacGILL	Yes it was, if they didn't write that down that's not my problem.
THOMAS	You saw the defendant pulling at a change tray.
OFFICER MacGILL	Check the tape. They taped the whole thing. I said it. I know I did.
THOMAS	You thought it was a gun.
OFFICER MacGILL	I didn't know what it was, but I...
THOMAS	Why did you think it was a gun?
OFFICER MacGILL	What do you mean?
THOMAS	He's pulling at something. Why did you think it was a gun?
OFFICER MacGILL	It... because...
THOMAS	It wasn't a gun, it was a change tray. You see a black person pulling at something in a car, why did you think it was a gun?

OFFICER MacGILL	He—he—okay—look, it's...
THOMAS	Answer the question.
OFFICER MacGILL	It's not as...
THOMAS	It's as simple as that. Yes it is. Answer the question.
OFFICER MacGILL	Okay, listen to me. The thing is... as an officer, I have the discretion to pull over anyone, of any colour...
THOMAS	Answer the question.
OFFICER MacGILL	...but you have to look at it from my perspective. I judged Mr. Moseby's behaviour to be suspicious. Not criminal, just suspicious. Weird. Based on what? Body movement, intensity. He was looking around furtively, as if he didn't want to be seen doing something. Now I'm not an idiot, I know some officers have crossed the line, racially. I don't think as many as the media would like us to believe. And if the problem was really that serious...
THOMAS	If?
OFFICER MacGILL	...then don't you think that...
THOMAS	If the problem is that serious? I WANT TO BE ABLE TO WALK DOWN THE STREET AND FEEL LIKE A CITIZEN OF THIS COUNTRY! That was taken away from me! Twice! Goddammit! I want to be able to walk down the street and... you know what? I want to be able to trust the police. I do. Thing is, I know I'm gonna get profiled again. Before I die. I know it!

And how does that make me feel? Funny you should ask. It makes me feel that the problem is systemic. It makes me think that judging people, based on race, is essential to policing. You wonder why Solomon won't just say who the shooter is? It's dead simple. It's not rocket science. You lie, they lie. You hide the truth, they hide the truth.

OFFICER MacGILL   I'm not hiding the truth.

THOMAS   Where was the gun?

OFFICER MacGILL   Sorry?

THOMAS   You found a gun in his possession. Where was it?

OFFICER MacGILL   In his pocket.

THOMAS   In his pocket. How did you find that out. How? It's in his pocket. You go to the car, you see he's pulling at a change tray, how do you know he's got a gun in his pocket? How? How!

OFFICER MacGILL thinks long and hard.

OFFICER MacGILL   If I do this, I lose my job.

THOMAS   Yes.

OFFICER MacGILL   I can't. I can't do it. I've got... my dad's got MS. I can't do it. Seriously. I can't.

THOMAS   Well, we'll just see about that.

OFFICER MacGILL   What do you mean?

THOMAS	Officer MacGill, non-compliance will have its repercussions.
OFFICER MacGILL	What does that mean?
THOMAS	You can go now. I have things to take care of.
OFFICER MacGILL	What repercussions?
THOMAS	Elsie. We're done. Could you leave my office please?

She leaves. Lights down on THOMAS. *Lights up on* SIMON, *he has a rose in his hand.*

SIMON knocks gently. ANGELIQUE *answers.*

ANGELIQUE	Simon?
SIMON	Hi, yeah, that's me.
ANGELIQUE	Come on in. Come on in.
SIMON	And this is...

He hands her the rose.

ANGELIQUE	Oh, that's so sweet! Oh my GOD! That's so nice of you.

She hugs him.

SIMON	I know it's really pathetic, but...
ANGELIQUE	No no no. It's so thoughtful. Thank you.
SIMON	So uhm.

ANGELIQUE	We should probably do the money thing first. Get that out of the way.
SIMON	Yes, I've got it right...
	Gives her an envelope.
ANGELIQUE	Thank you very much.
SIMON	And what's your name again?
ANGELIQUE	Angelique.
SIMON	Ah. Okay. That's... that's a beautiful name.
ANGELIQUE	Yeah, well, I had to pick something and it's like... I don't know. I just had to pick something.
SIMON	Is it totally wrong of me to ask what your real name is?
ANGELIQUE	Well, you can ask...
SIMON	Fine. Sorry.
ANGELIQUE	Let me take your coat.
SIMON	Oh, no, I can do that.
	He takes his coat off.
ANGELIQUE	And I really have to apologize, I'm so sorry but I had a cigarette right before you got here.
SIMON	Don't worry about it.

ANGELIQUE	I'm so sorry.
SIMON	No, seriously, don't... I used to smoke and...
ANGELIQUE	How'd you quit? Let me know, I'm ready to try anything.
SIMON	Oh I had to quit everything. Drinking, cigarettes, pot, coke. Everything. But if you want to smoke around me you can.
ANGELIQUE	Are you sure?
SIMON	Actually I find it... it's kinda...
ANGELIQUE	Yeah.
SIMON	Can I... can... is it okay if I... if I kiss you?
ANGELIQUE	This is your first time, isn't it?
SIMON	Can you tell?
ANGELIQUE	No kissing on the mouth or the vagina, everywhere else is fine.
SIMON	Okay.
ANGELIQUE	And nothing happens without a...

SIMON pulls a condom out of his pocket.

Good for you.

SIMON	May I kiss your neck?
ANGELIQUE	Yes you may.

He pulls her to him, softly, kisses her neck passionately.

SIMON   This is uhm.... You are so beautiful, and... this is really...

He tries to kiss her mouth.

ANGELIQUE   Simon. Simon. Not the mouth, okay? Not... SIMON...

SIMON   Just, PLEASE, just once, PLEASE...

ANGELIQUE   Simon...

He pulls at her roughly. They struggle.

SIMON   Is it the money? Do you need more money? Come on... just...

His phone rings. She pushes him off. Awkward silence.

ANGELIQUE   Are you gonna get that?

SIMON looks at the number.

SIMON   Hello? What? Well, okay. Uhm... I'll be right there.

He hangs up.

ANGELIQUE   You gotta go?

SIMON   Yeah, I gotta go.

ANGELIQUE   Okay, well...

	SIMON collects his things.
SIMON	I'm sorry, I uh...
ANGELIQUE	Don't sweat it. Seriously.
	SIMON exits. Lights down on ANGELIQUE. Lights up on THOMAS.
THOMAS	Squat, red-brick buildings. Smashed in windows covered with boards. And of course the thought strikes me: I can't tell her I didn't mean it. 'Cause even if I didn't mean it she's gonna still wonder why I said it and I said it because... I don't know why I said it, I do and I don't, and am I going the right direction? Twenty-five B. That should be over here. Simon's not here yet. Perfect. Rose? Hi, I'm Thomas Matthews.
ROSE	Eh.
THOMAS	I see you got my message.
ROSE	I don't understand how this should involve me?
	SIMON enters.
SIMON	What the hell are you doing?!
THOMAS	Ah, there you are.
SIMON	You don't talk to my client!
THOMAS	She's not your client, she's the sister of your client.

SIMON	She's my client! Don't talk to her.
ROSE	It's all right, Mr. Simon. I can take care of myself.
SIMON	I know, I know, I just.... What's going on?
THOMAS	I've got a meeting with a police association rep in about forty minutes. We're gonna draft something that Officer MacGill can sign confessing to racially profiling your client.
SIMON	And...
THOMAS	But before I can do that, I want to talk to Solomon.
SIMON	You want to what?
THOMAS	I just want to talk to the kid. Have a few words. I want to get a sense of where his head is at. I want to know that he's worth it.
SIMON	You want... you...
THOMAS	I understand what I'm asking for is uncon...
SIMON	Okay, you know what? I realize you don't listen to a word I say, and that's fine. But I really, really want you to pay attention to everything I'm about to tell you. And I really need you to focus, okay? Now. You feel guilt. Fine.
THOMAS	I don't f...
SIMON	That's okay. Guilt is good. It means you're human, and that's great. However, the place

that Solomon Mosbey is in right now, in his life, has nothing to do with your guilt.

ROSE   Mr. Simon, I...

THOMAS   What does it have to do with?

SIMON   Social programs in this province...

THOMAS   Oh God...

SIMON   ...in this province have been slashed to bits!

THOMAS   Everyone has choices.

SIMON   No, you don't have a choice! You don't! Not if you're starving! You don't!

THOMAS   Don't you dare try and tell me that anyone in this entire country has any idea what it really means to be starving, to be poor. You go to Darfur, you go to the streets of Nigeria, and you tell me that any poor person in this entire continent has a clue about what it means to be truly hungry, to be...

SIMON   You know what I frickin hate about all you frickin neo-con frickin assholes?

THOMAS   What the...?!

SIMON   The thing about you and your pal Stephen Harper...

THOMAS   Oh hohoho...

SIMON   The "Christian" prime minister, the thing about him, and you and all you guys, is that

you want the poor to prove their moral
worth.

THOMAS   Is that so?

SIMON   As if Mr. James Flaherty, the Antichrist, the
                freakin Nazi, as if he wasn't responsible for
                dumping thousands of people off welfare and
                onto the street!

THOMAS   Wow. You know what drives me up the freak-
                ing wall about you NDP, left-wing freaking
                nut jobs?

SIMON   Tell me. Love to hear it.

THOMAS   Guys like you and Jack Layton abandon Bob
                Rae, and Harris gets into power, and surprise,
                surprise, he destroys every social policy your
                precious NDP was trying to protect. Now why
                did he do that? Oh, that's right. Because he
                said he would! And so now your beloved Jack
                Layton is out of a job, oh no, that's right. He's
                leader of the federal NDP, and what's he do-
                ing? Bitching and complaining from inside a
                party that will never hold power! Come down
                off that high horse of yours. You're gonna get
                a nosebleed up there. Give me a call when you
                do.

                THOMAS leaves.

ROSE   You know, Mister Simon. Me tink we gonna
                need ta finish dis soon.

                *ROSE leaves. Lights down on SIMON. Lights
                up on ALMANDA on the phone.*

ALMANDA	Hello, I'm... this is Mrs. Matthews calling from Parkdale CI. I'm leaving a message, uh, I didn't see Violet here today, she was supposed to meet with me this afternoon, and... I'll be here for another twenty minutes, if... you get this message. Thank you.
	She hangs up.
	Perfect. I should... now I'm just searching for any excuse not to go home. I'm dreading the inevitable, the confrontation, the... and... and I think I catch a glimpse of someone staring at me, a male, young, at the door. I don't recognize him. He's standing outside, looking in. He's not one of my students. I've never seen him at this school before. Should I... is he... he's coming in. I get to the...
	CHORUS 6, as YOUNG MALE in a hoodie, face obscured, walks up to her slowly. She's scared.
YOUNG MALE	Yo, you Violet's teacher?
ALMANDA	What...
YOUNG MALE	Yo, listen, Violet don't be comin round here no mo.
ALMANDA	Why?
YOUNG MALE	Someone shot up her front yard. Her mom's moved they shit someplace else. She ain't comin back.
ALMANDA	Okay.

YOUNG MALE	But she wanted me to thank you for tryin'.
ALMANDA	She what?
YOUNG MALE	She say she wants me to thank you for trying to help.
ALMANDA	So... all right. Well. Uh... thank you.
YOUNG MALE	Peace.

He is about to leave.

ALMANDA	Tell her... tell her that... tell her good luck.

The YOUNG MALE leaves. Lights down on ALMANDA. Lights up on THOMAS, SIMON, OFFICER MacGILL, and ROSE. THOMAS has the affidavit.

SIMON	...what was that? No. No, the kids are fine. They miss you. Yes they do. I gotta go. I'm sorry, how was Passover? How... honey, how was Passover? Yeah?

THOMAS clears his throat.

Great. That's great. I've... I've got to go. I've got to go. I can't do this every single time we... you're gonna be home Saturday. I'll pick you up at the train station. The kids are fine. Yes I will. You won't have to wait. I promise. I love you too. Kay. Bye. Bye. Bye.

THOMAS	Can we get this over and done with?
SIMON	Sorry about that.

THOMAS	I don't have all day.
SIMON	You know, I uh... I meant what I said about respecting people who do your job.
THOMAS	Is he far?
SIMON	What?
THOMAS	Solomon. What room is he in?
SIMON	He's just around the corner.

THOMAS offers the affidavit.

| THOMAS | I wanna see him. |
| SIMON | He's sleeping. |

THOMAS pulls away the affidavit.

THOMAS	Wake him up.
SIMON	I... that's not a good idea. Can I...
THOMAS	Are you kidding me? I need the name.
SIMON	You'll get it. Give me the...
THOMAS	When?
SIMON	When he wakes up. Give me the affidavit.
THOMAS	When is that?
SIMON	Soon. Thomas... the affidavit please. The affidavit? Thomas.

THOMAS starts to clue in.

THOMAS   You son of a bitch.

OFFICER MacGILL   What?

THOMAS   He's not conscious, is he?

SIMON   Not yet.

THOMAS   Oh for...

SIMON   He will be. When he is, you'll get your name. Now give me the...

THOMAS   How long has he been out?

SIMON   Since he came in. He's in stable condition. He's going to get better, he's getting better, it's just a...

THOMAS   You son of a bitch.

SIMON   He's gonna get better. And when he does get better, when he comes to, you can expect a full...

THOMAS   I want to see him.

SIMON   What?

THOMAS   I want to see him.

SIMON   Why?

THOMAS   I want to see him, GODDAMNIT! Why? I don't know why. Maybe I... I just ..

THOMAS turns to ROSE.

Can I see him? Can I do that, please? Please.

SIMON   Rose?

ROSE   Yeah. Sure.

THOMAS leaves. OFFICER MacGILL walks over to ROSE.

OFFICER MacGILL   I hope your brother pulls through.

ROSE   Don't you talk to me. You never talk to me. Unnastand?

OFFICER MacGILL leaves. ROSE leaves. Lights down on SIMON. Lights up on SOLOMON.

SOLOMON   And the walls start to flicker a little bit. I can remember that I'm at a hospital. But that goes in and out. And I know my sister is by my side, and she whispers to me...

ROSE   My warrior. My African prince.

SOLOMON   ...but I start to do that thing where you say the word over and over again and it becomes alien and meaningless and I start to wonder what a sister is. And then the thought shifts sideways and becomes a wall and I realize the room is getting bigger and bigger. My hands are getting bigger and heavier, I can't even lift them anymore. And I just want to let my head fall to the side because it's so heavy and it's now huge and above me and I'm sinking...

CHORUS 2	Ten to the minus one centimetres.
SOLOMON	It's not falling, it's like shifting, sliding. And it's warm. And it was dark, but now I can make out shapes of some kind...
CHORUS 3	Ten to the minus eight centimetres.
SOLOMON	I was gonna say it's like being high, but it's not. It's like nothing I've ever experienced but it reminds me of sex, of losing and gaining and being, and not, all at once, and I'm...
CHORUS 4	Ten to the minus twelve centimetres.
SOLOMON	An insignificance. I'm the whole universe and nothing all at the same time. And I'm spreading out. I'm getting thinner.
CHORUS 5	Ten to the minus sixteen.
SOLOMON	And then suddenly...
CHORUS 6	Ten to the minus seventeen.
SOLOMON	...as it I was dropped into a sea of daggers...
CHORUS 2	Ten to the minus eighteen.
SOLOMON	I never thought I could ever get this thin. I'm spreading out. Leaking. I'm into everything now. I'm in you. I'm in your consciousness. I'm floating around your consciousness. I am sinking into the oblivion of your consciousness. I was the size of a positron, but now I'm not even that.
CHORUS 3	Ten to the minus twenty.

SOLOMON	Massive, gargantuan strings tied to this universe, rippling in vibrations like ropes tied to the mast of a ship in a hurricane, hold this universe to a colossal...
CHORUS 4	Ten to the minus twenty-five.
SOLOMON	What the hell is that?!
CHORUS 5	Ten to the minus twenty-seven.
SOLOMON	I can see the horizon...
CHORUS 6	Ten to the minus twenty-eight.
SOLOMON	I can feel the horizon.
CHORUS 2	Ten to the minus twenty-nine.
	She holds her hands slightly apart.
SOLOMON	Tearing me apart!
CHORUS 3	Ten to the minus thirty.
SOLOMON	Vaporizing me!
CHORUS 4	Ten to the minus thirty-one.
SOLOMON	Ahhhh!
CHORUS 5	Ten to the minus thirty-two.
SOLOMON	It hurts!
CHORUS 6	Ten to the minus thirty-three.
	SOLOMON screams at the top of his lungs.

SOLOMON	Aaaaaaaaaaaaahhhh!

As he does this, CHORUS 2 *closes her hands together. When her hands touch he stops screaming.*

SIMON	I'm walking.
ROSE	One foot after the other.
THOMAS	And then I sit down...
SIMON	I lean...
ROSE	Over the table. My tears are so hot.
OFFICER MACGILL	My mind lost in a hundred thousand personal things.

OFFICER MACGILL *looking at the affidavit.*

ALMANDA	I know he's home...
ROSE	It's still too cold to have people get together outside...
OFFICER MACGILL	Out along Dundas, left on University...
ALMANDA	And I stand outside for a while. To collect my...
THOMAS	And I should be making myself look busy. But I sit there, on the couch, flicking my finger against my knee, and I can hear the door open.
ROSE	Standing in front of people I don't even know. And all these young men, boys, looking so lost, so lost...

OFFICER MacGILL tears up the affidavit.

OFFICER MacGILL   Right on Gerrard. Tip my hat to a woman walking her dog.

SIMON   And here I am.

ALMANDA   My throat is dry, my hands are sweating…

SIMON   Self-medicating and taking it one step at a time.

THOMAS   So she says to me…

ALMANDA   And I'm trying to say all the things in my head the way I want to say them.

THOMAS   So I try to make a joke about how even if I was with a black woman she would still scream at me about the licence sticker and it really doesn't go that well at all.

ALMANDA   We walk past Grappa on College.

THOMAS   But it allows her to look at me as being that typical male who doesn't get it and…

OFFICER MacGILL   Look at that sky.

ALMANDA   Waiters busy shuffling food into the mouths of the elite of the city.

OFFICER MacGILL   Look at that sky.

THOMAS and ALMANDA sit and hold each other.

THOMAS   And I tell her that I didn't mean it, because that's all I've got, and I have to say it. I do.

ALMANDA   And I'm explaining my hurt, my... explaining how I feel, as one does in this situation, and as my emotions are fluctuating, undulating, I'm thinking, I really hope our child has his eyes, I really do. Look at his... God. Look at his eyes.

THOMAS   It was a thought that was never supposed to be said out loud.

ALMANDA   And when we get to the Metro, a brisk breeze cuts into our step and we stroll a little slower. And I start to think... I'm going to live and die in this city, aren't I?

THOMAS   Some things...

ALMANDA   I'm gonna raise a family and live and die here.

THOMAS   Lots of things, you don't say out loud.

           They hold each other. He is behind her, they both face the audience.

ALMANDA   And my child is going to discover all those crazy, enigmatic intricacies of the external world and all the wild absurdities of their inner life and there are worse places on the planet to do that, I suppose.

THOMAS   That's just the way it is.

ALMANDA   I lean back, the CN Tower's shining in the night sky, pointing to some far-off destination in the universe, out into infinity.

Lights down. SIMON *enters with a package, knocks.*

SIMON   Hey.

THOMAS   What do you want?

SIMON   May I uh... may I come in?

THOMAS   You've got two minutes.

SIMON   I uhm... my wife's coming in on the train. I thought, hell, I'm in the neighbourhood...

           SIMON shows THOMAS a picture of his children on his iPhone.

           This is Rebecca, and this is Sarah.

THOMAS   Cute.

SIMON   Damn right they are.

           He gives THOMAS a package.

THOMAS   What's this?

SIMON   Some of it is new. Some not so much.

THOMAS   Oh now look what you did.

SIMON   I was gonna sell it all on Craigslist, but then I thought of you and...

THOMAS   Right. Okay.

SIMON   And this is the only bath seat you will ever want. You fill the kitchen sink with warm

	water, you put the kid in here. The big plastic tubs, they're more trouble than they're worth. Trust me.
THOMAS	Got it.
SIMON	I should go. I have to pick my wife up at the train station.
THOMAS	Okay.
SIMON	I hated moving here. I hated it. At first. I'd just graduated from UBC, and uh... I get here and all the bars closed at one a.m. and that just killed me. And Vancouver has this epic beauty...
THOMAS	When it's not raining.
SIMON	Yeah, well. Yeah. And everyone here was just so... so cold and distant and... but I'm here. And a friend takes me out to a speakeasy, and they've got "How Soon Is Now" blaring on the turntable, and I decide to get some fresh air...

He mimes a cigarette with his hand to suggest that what he means is he went for a smoke.

...and it's four a.m., and I'm looking out over the city and no one's out on the street, the sun's about to come up, and there was... a serenity. A serenity that... I don't know if I'm projecting this, or if I'm... I don't know. There, there was a... tranquility, a peace that... whatever. Anyway. I should...

SIMON starts to leave.

THOMAS	There's a tiny little parking lot on the west side of Union Station just south of Front.
SIMON	Oh yeah?
THOMAS	Dip down to Lakeshore. Go up York. It's hard to see. Nobody knows about it. Nobody's ever there unless the Leafs are playing. Tiny little lot right at the station. So you don't have to go and park all the way down at the Air Canada Centre.
SIMON	And Thomas?
THOMAS	Yeah?
SIMON	If you ever get profiled…
THOMAS	Dude, you're at the top of my list.
SIMON	Good. Good.

SIMON leaves.

THOMAS	I grab my things. Head out the door. Start walking east towards the parking lot on Dundas. Looks like it's going to rain.

The End

Andrew Moodie exploded onto the theatre scene in 1995 with his first play, *Riot*. Since then he has been a mainstay of Canadian television and theatre, both as an actor and as a writer. His other plays include *Oui*, *A Common Man's Guide to Loving Women*, and *The Real McCoy*.